BALLADS AND POEMS

1915-1930

WORKS OF

STEPHEN VINCENT BENÉT

❧

THE BEGINNING OF WISDOM

FIVE MEN AND POMPEY

JOHN BROWN'S BODY

YOUNG PEOPLE'S PRIDE

HEAVENS AND EARTH

SPANISH BAYONET

YOUNG ADVENTURE

JEAN HUGUENOT

TIGER JOY

BALLADS AND POEMS
1915-1930

BALLADS

and POEMS

1915·1930

STEPHEN VINCENT

BENÉT

DOUBLEDAY, DORAN & COMPANY, INC.

Garden City 1931 New York

PRINTED AT THE *Country Life Press*, GARDEN CITY, N. Y., U. S. A.

TO ROSEMARY

If you were gone afar,
And lost the pattern
Of all your delightful ways,
And the web undone,
How would one make you anew,
From what dew and flowers,
What burning and mingled atoms,
Under the sun?

Not from too-satin roses,
Or those rare blossoms,
Orchids, scentless and precious
As precious stone.
But out of lemon-verbena,
Rose-geranium,
These alone.

Not with running horses,
Or Spanish cannon,
Organs, voiced like a lion,
Clamor and speed.
But perhaps with old music-boxes,

Young, tawny kittens,
Wild-strawberry-seed.

Even so, it were more
Than a god could compass
To fashion the body merely,
The lovely shroud.
But then—ah, how to recapture
That evanescence,
The fire that cried in pure crystal
Out of its cloud!

NOTE

This book is, in the main, a selection from three earlier books of verse, all now out of print. Some new poems have been added and certain old ones altered, though not materially—one cannot rewrite, after fifteen years, without changing the work completely. The earliest poems in this book were written in 1915, the latest in 1930.

"The Island and the Fire" was read, as the Phi Beta Kappa poem, before the Harvard chapter, June, 1930.

S. V. B.

New York City, 1930

CONTENTS

xi

I AMERICAN NAMES

AMERICAN NAMES

I HAVE fallen in love with American names,
The sharp names that never get fat,
The snakeskin-titles of mining-claims,
The plumed war-bonnet of Medicine Hat,
Tucson and Deadwood and Lost Mule Flat.

Seine and Piave are silver spoons,
But the spoonbowl-metal is thin and worn,
There are English counties like hunting-tunes
Played on the keys of a postboy's horn,
But I will remember where I was born.

I will remember Carquinez Straits,
Little French Lick and Lundy's Lane,
The Yankee ships and the Yankee dates
And the bullet-towns of Calamity Jane.
I will remember Skunktown Plain.

[3]

I will fall in love with a Salem tree
And a rawhide quirt from Santa Cruz,
I will get me a bottle of Boston sea
And a blue-gum nigger to sing me blues.
I am tired of loving a foreign muse.

Rue des Martyrs and Bleeding-Heart-Yard,
Senlis, Pisa, and Blindman's Oast,
It is a magic ghost you guard
But I am sick for a newer ghost,
Harrisburg, Spartanburg, Painted Post.

Henry and John were never so
And Henry and John were always right?
Granted, but when it was time to go
And the tea and the laurels had stood all night,
Did they never watch for Nantucket Light?

I shall not rest quiet in Montparnasse.
I shall not lie easy at Winchelsea.
You may bury my body in Sussex grass,
You may bury my tongue at Champmédy.
I shall not be there. I shall rise and pass.
Bury my heart at Wounded Knee.

THE BALLAD
OF WILLIAM SYCAMORE

(1790–1871)

MY FATHER, he was a mountaineer,
His fist was a knotty hammer;
He was quick on his feet as a running deer,
And he spoke with a Yankee stammer.

My mother, she was merry and brave,
And so she came to her labor,
With a tall green fir for her doctor grave
And a stream for her comforting neighbor.

And some are wrapped in the linen fine,
And some like a godling's scion;
But I was cradled on twigs of pine
In the skin of a mountain lion.

And some remember a white, starched lap
And a ewer with silver handles;
But I remember a coonskin cap
And the smell of bayberry candles.

[5]

The cabin logs, with the bark still rough,
And my mother who laughed at trifles,
And the tall, lank visitors, brown as snuff,
With their long, straight squirrel-rifles.

I can hear them dance, like a foggy song,
Through the deepest one of my slumbers,
The fiddle squeaking the boots along
And my father calling the numbers.

The quick feet shaking the puncheon-floor,
And the fiddle squealing and squealing,
Till the dried herbs rattled above the door
And the dust went up to the ceiling.

There are children lucky from dawn till dusk,
But never a child so lucky!
For I cut my teeth on "Money Musk"
In the Bloody Ground of Kentucky!

When I grew tall as the Indian corn,
My father had little to lend me,
But he gave me his great, old powder-horn
And his woodsman's skill to befriend me.

With a leather shirt to cover my back,
And a redskin nose to unravel
Each forest sign, I carried my pack
As far as a scout could travel.

Till I lost my boyhood and found my wife,
A girl like a Salem clipper!
A woman straight as a hunting-knife
With eyes as bright as the Dipper!

We cleared our camp where the buffalo feed,
Unheard-of streams were our flagons;
And I sowed my sons like the apple-seed
On the trail of the Western wagons.

They were right, tight boys, never sulky or slow,
A fruitful, a goodly muster.
The eldest died at the Alamo.
The youngest fell with Custer.

The letter that told it burned my hand.
Yet we smiled and said, "So be it!"
But I could not live when they fenced the land,
For it broke my heart to see it.

I saddled a red, unbroken colt
And rode him into the day there;
And he threw me down like a thunderbolt
And rolled on me as I lay there.

The hunter's whistle hummed in my ear
As the city-men tried to move me,
And I died in my boots like a pioneer
With the whole wide sky above me.

Now I lie in the heart of the fat, black soil,
Like the seed of a prairie-thistle;
It has washed my bones with honey and oil
And picked them clean as a whistle.

And my youth returns, like the rains of Spring,
And my sons, like the wild-geese flying;
And I lie and hear the meadow-lark sing
And have much content in my dying.

Go play with the towns you have built of blocks,
The towns where you would have bound me!
I sleep in my earth like a tired fox,
And my buffalo have found me.

THE HEMP

I. The Planting of the Hemp

CAPTAIN HAWK *scourged clean the seas*
(Black is the gap below the plank)
From the Great North Bank to the Caribbees.
(Down by the marsh the hemp grows rank).

His fear was on the seaport towns,
The weight of his hand held hard the downs.

And the merchants cursed him, bitter and black,
For a red flame in the sea-fog's wrack
Was all of their ships that might come back.

For all he had one word alone,
One clod of dirt in their faces thrown,
"The hemp that shall hang me is not grown!"

[9]

His name bestrode the seas like Death,
The waters trembled at his breath.

This is the tale of how he fell,
Of the long sweep and the heavy swell,
And the rope that dragged him down to hell.

The fight was done, and the gutted ship,
Stripped like a shark the sea-gulls strip,

Lurched blindly, eaten out with flame,
Back to the land from whence she came,
A skimming horror, an eyeless shame.

And Hawk stood up on his quarter-deck,
And saw the sky and saw the wreck.

Below, a butt for sailors' jeers,
White as the sky when a white squall nears,
Huddled the crowd of the prisoners.

Over the bridge of the tottering plank,
Where the sea shook and the gulf yawned blank,
They shrieked and struggled and dropped and sank.

Pinioned arms and hands bound fast.
One girl alone was left at last.

Sir Henry Gaunt was a mighty lord.
He sat in state at the Council board.

The governors were as naught to him.
From one rim to the other rim

Of his great plantations, flung out wide
Like a purple cloak, was a full month's ride.

Life and death in his white hands lay,
And his only daughter stood at bay,
Trapped like a hare in the toils that day.

He sat at wine in his gold and his lace,
And far away, in a bloody place,
Hawk came near, and she covered her face.

He rode in the fields, and the hunt was brave,
And far away, his daughter gave
A shriek that the seas cried out to hear,
And he could not see and he could not save.

Her white soul withered in the mire
As paper shrivels up in fire,
And Hawk laughed, and he kissed her mouth,
And her body he took for his desire.

THE HEMP

II. The Growing of the Hemp

Sir Henry stood in the manor room,
And his eyes were hard gems in the gloom.

And he said, "Go, dig me furrows five
Where the green marsh creeps like a thing alive—
There at its edge where the rushes thrive."

And where the furrows rent the ground
He sowed the seed of hemp around.

And the blacks shrink back and are sore afraid
At the furrows five that rib the glade,
And the voodoo work of the master's spade.

For a cold wind blows from the marshland near,
And white things move, and the night grows drear,
And they chatter and crouch and are sick with fear.

[12]

But down by the marsh, where the grey slaves glean,
The hemp sprouts up, and the earth is seen
Veiled with a tenuous mist of green.

And Hawk still scourges the Caribbees,
And many men kneel at his knees.

Sir Henry sits in his house alone,
And his eyes are hard and dull like stone.

And the waves beat, and the winds roar,
And all things are as they were before.

And the days pass, and the weeks pass,
And nothing changes but the grass.

But down where the fireflies are like eyes,
And the damps shudder, and the mists rise,
The hemp-stalks stand up toward the skies.

And down from the poop of the pirate ship
A body falls, and the great sharks grip.

Innocent, lovely, go in grace!
At last there is peace upon your face.

And Hawk laughs loud as the corpse is thrown,
"The hemp that shall hang me is not grown!"

Sir Henry's face is iron to mark,
And he gazes ever in the dark.

And the days pass, and the weeks pass,
And the world is as it always was.

But down by the marsh the sickles beam,
Glitter on glitter, gleam on gleam,
And the hemp falls down by the stagnant stream.

And Hawk beats up from the Caribbees,
Swooping to pounce in the Northern seas.

Sir Henry sits sunk deep in his chair,
And white as his hand is grown his hair.

And the days pass, and the weeks pass,
And the sands roll from the hourglass.

But down by the marsh, in the blazing sun,
The hemp is smoothed and twisted and spun.
The rope made, and the work done.

THE HEMP

III. *The Using of the Hemp*

Captain Hawk scourged clean the seas,
(Black is the gap below the plank)
From the Great North Bank to the Caribbees
(Down by the marsh the hemp grows rank)

He sailed in the broad Atlantic track
And the ships that saw him came not back.

Till once again, where the wide tides ran,
He stopped to harry a merchantman.

He bade her stop.   Ten guns spoke true
From her hidden ports, and a hidden crew,
Lacking his great ship through and through.

Dazed and dumb with the sudden death,
He scarce had time to draw a breath

[15]

Before the grappling-irons bit deep
And the boarders slew his crew like sheep.

Hawk stood up straight, his breast to the steel;
His cutlass made a bloody wheel.

His cutlass made a wheel of flame.
They shrank before him as he came.

And the bodies fell in a choking crowd,
And still he thundered out aloud,

"The hemp that shall hang me is not grown!"
They fled at last. He was left alone.

Before his foe Sir Henry stood.
"The hemp is grown and my word made good!"

And the cutlass clanged with a hissing whir
On the lashing blade of the rapier.

Hawk roared and charged like a maddened buck.
As the cobra strikes, Sir Henry struck,

Pouring his life in a single thrust,
And the cutlass shivered to sparks and dust.

Sir Henry stood on the blood-stained deck,
And set his foot on his foe's neck.

Then, from the hatch, where the torn decks slope,
Where the dead roll and the wounded grope,
He dragged the serpent of the rope.

The sky was blue and the sea was still,
The waves lapped softly, hill on hill,
And between one wave and another wave
The doomed man's cries were little and shrill.

The sea was blue and the sky was calm,
The air dripped with a golden balm.
Like a wind-blown fruit between sea and sun,
A black thing writhed at a yard-arm.

Slowly then, and awesomely,
The ship sank, and the gallows-tree,
And there was nought between sea and sun—
Nought but the sun and the sky and the sea.

But down by the marsh, where the fever breeds,
Only the water chuckles and pleads;
For the hemp clings fast to a dead man's throat,
And blind Fate gathers back her seeds.

THE MOUNTAIN WHIPPOORWILL

OR, HOW HILL-BILLY JIM WON THE GREAT FIDDLERS' PRIZE

(*A Georgia Romance*)

Up in the mountains, it's lonesome all the time,
(Sof' win' slewin' thu' the sweet-potato vine).

Up in the mountains, it's lonesome for a child,
(Whippoorwills a-callin' when the sap runs wild).

Up in the mountains, mountains in the fog,
Everythin's as lazy as an old houn' dog.

Born in the mountains, never raised a pet,
Don't want nuthin' an' never got it yet.

Born in the mountains, lonesome-born,
Raised runnin' ragged thu' the cockleburrs and corn.

Never knew my pappy, mebbe never should.
Think he was a fiddle made of mountain laurel-wood.

[18]

Never had a mammy to teach me pretty-please.
Think she was a whippoorwill, a-skitin' thu' the trees.

Never had a brother ner a whole pair of pants,
But when I start to fiddle, why, yuh got to start to dance!

Listen to my fiddle—Kingdom Come—Kingdom Come!
Hear the frogs a-chunkin' "Jug o' rum, Jug o' rum!"
Hear that mountain-whippoorwill be lonesome in the air,
An' I'll tell yuh how I traveled to the Essex County Fair.

Essex County has a mighty pretty fair,
All the smarty fiddlers from the South come there.

Elbows flyin' as they rosin up the bow
For the First Prize Contest in the Georgia Fiddlers' Show.

Old Dan Wheeling, with his whiskers in his ears,
King-pin fiddler for nearly twenty years.

Big Tom Sargent, with his blue wall-eye,
An' Little Jimmy Weezer that can make a fiddle cry.

All sittin' roun', spittin' high an' struttin' proud,
(Listen, little whippoorwill, yuh better bug yore eyes!)
Tun-a-tun-a-tunin' while the jedges told the crowd
Them that got the mostest claps'd win the bestest prize.

Everybody waitin' for the first tweedle-dee,
When in comes a-stumblin'—hill-billy me!

Bowed right pretty to the jedges an' the rest,
Took a silver dollar from a hole inside my vest,

Plunked it on the table an' said, "There's my callin' card!
An' anyone that licks me—well, he's got to fiddle hard!"

Old Dan Wheeling, he was laughin' fit to holler,
Little Jimmy Weezer said, "There's one dead dollar!"

Big Tom Sargent had a yaller-toothy grin,
But I tucked my little whippoorwill spang underneath my
    chin,
An' petted it an' tuned it till the jedges said, "Begin!"

Big Tom Sargent was the first in line;
He could fiddle all the bugs off a sweet-potato vine.
He could fiddle down a possum from a mile-high tree.
He could fiddle up a whale from the bottom of the sea.

Yuh could hear hands spankin' till they spanked each
    other raw,
When he finished variations on "Turkey in the Straw."

Little Jimmy Weezer was the next to play;
He could fiddle all night, he could fiddle all day.

He could fiddle chills, he could fiddle fever,
He could make a fiddle rustle like a lowland river.

He could make a fiddle croon like a lovin' woman.
An' they clapped like thunder when he'd finished
    strummin'.

Then came the ruck of the bob-tailed fiddlers,
The let's go-easies, the fair-to-middlers.

They got their claps an' they lost their bicker,
An' settled back for some more corn-licker.

An' the crowd was tired of their no-count squealing,
When out in the center steps Old Dan Wheeling.

He fiddled high and he fiddled low,
(Listen, little whippoorwill; yuh got to spread yore wings!)
He fiddled with a cherrywood bow.
(Old Dan Wheeling's got bee-honey in his strings.)

He fiddled the wind by the lonesome moon,
He fiddled a most almighty tune.

He started fiddling like a ghost,
He ended fiddling like a host.

He fiddled north an' he fiddled south,
He fiddled the heart right out of yore mouth.

He fiddled here an' he fiddled there.
He fiddled salvation everywhere.

When he was finished, the crowd cut loose,
(Whippoorwill, they's rain on yore breast.)
An' I sat there wonderin', "What's the use?"
(Whippoorwill, fly home to yore nest.)

But I stood up pert an' I took my bow,
An' my fiddle went to my shoulder, so.

An'—they wasn't no crowd to get me fazed—
But I was alone where I was raised.

Up in the mountains, so still it makes yuh skeered.
Where God lies sleepin' in his big white beard.

An' I heard the sound of the squirrel in the pine,
An' I heard the earth a-breathin' thu' the long night-time.

They've fiddled the rose, an' they've fiddled the thorn,
But they haven't fiddled the mountain-corn.

They've fiddled sinful an' fiddled moral,
But they haven't fiddled the breshwood-laurel.

They've fiddled loud, an' they've fiddled still,
But they haven't fiddled the whippoorwill.

I started off with a *dump-diddle-dump*,
(*Oh, hell's broke loose in Georgia!*)
Skunk-cabbage growin' by the bee-gum stump,
(*Whippoorwill, yo're singin' now!*)

Oh, Georgia booze is mighty fine booze,
The best yuh ever poured yuh,
But it eats the soles right offen yore shoes,
For Hell's broke loose in Georgia.

My mother was a whippoorwill pert,
My father, he was lazy,
But I'm Hell broke loose in a new store shirt
To fiddle all Georgia crazy.

Swing yore partners—up an' down the middle!
Sashay now—oh, listen to that fiddle!
Flapjacks flippin' on a red-hot griddle,

An' hell broke loose,
Hell broke loose,
Fire on the mountains—snakes in the grass.
Satan's here a-bilin'—oh, Lordy, let him pass!
Go down Moses, set my people free,
Pop goes the weasel thu' the old Red Sea!
Jonah sittin' on a hickory-bough,
Up jumps a whale—an' where's yore prophet now?
Rabbit in the pea-patch, possum in the pot,
Try an' stop my fiddle, now my fiddle's gettin' hot!
Whippoorwill, singin' thu' the mountain hush,
Whippoorwill, shoutin' from the burnin' bush,
Whippoorwill, cryin' in the stable-door,
Sing to-night as yuh never sang before!
Hell's broke loose like a stompin' mountain-shoat,
Sing till yuh bust the gold in yore throat!
Hell's broke loose for forty miles aroun'
Bound to stop yore music if yuh don't sing it down.
Sing on the mountains, little whippoorwill,
Sing to the valleys, an' slap 'em with a hill,
For I'm struttin' high as an eagle's quill,
An' Hell's broke loose,
Hell's broke loose,
Hell's broke loose in Georgia!

They wasn't a sound when I stopped bowin',
(*Whippoorwill, yuh can sing no more.*)
But, somewhere or other, the dawn was growin',
(*Oh, mountain whippoorwill!*)

An' I thought, "I've fiddled all night an' lost.
Yo're a good hill-billy, but yuh've been bossed."

So I went to congratulate old man Dan,
—But he put his fiddle into my han'—
An' then the noise of the crowd began.

MOON-ISLAND

*(Deposition of Christopher Hew,
the Last American Pirate)*

WHEN we first sighted land
How it made our hearts thunder
To think of new plunder
Dropped into our hand!
When we first sighted land.

It was Midsummer Day
When we let go the anchor,
But the sun had no rancor
Within that calm bay.

We rowed to its shores
With our muskets beside us
And a devil to ride us
With red-hot moidores.

[24]

But the beach was so white,
And the slow minutes crept,
And the hot devil slept,
And the moon rose, in light,

Frail as nautilus shell,
And somehow—in our souls—
We forgot we were coals
Half rejected by hell.

We had come there to loot,
But we sprawled and grew tame there.
And brown women came there
With baskets of fruit.

Fruit cold as moonshine
With a strange taste, and sweet,
With a taste that could beat
Any Portugal wine.

They kept singing a tune,
And we ate—and we gaped—
For each fruitseed was shaped
Like a little new moon.

2

Then we drowsed without care
For our devil was gone,
And the singing kept on,
And the moon filled the air.

And we did not go back
To our ship in the bay,
To our old bird of prey
Where the Roger flapped slack,
And we had the arrack.

No, we lingered and stayed,
And time passed like the sleep
Yellow emperors keep
In their coffins of jade,

While we swam in the pool
Or we played knucklebones
Or we skipped little stones
Like boys out of school.

By the gold hands of day
And the silver of night
We were coins scoured bright
And our sins fell away.

We were wasps without stings,
We were children again there.
Oh, we could have been men there!
We could have been kings.

3

On the last night of all
The moon was at full,
And we heard the tide pull
At the beach's pale shawl.

And the moonseeds had grown
As the moon grew in size,
Till like round silver eyes
In the dark fruit they shone.

And we ate, and the tune
That the brown women sang
Gathered and rang
In a heathenish croon,

As we tossed out the seeds
For the moonbeams to bleach
On the long, burnished beach
Like a goddess's beads.

And then—was it a dream
Or the wine of the fruit?
The moonseeds took root
Where the light made them gleam.

And the roots grew and swelled
And were quickened to vine
In the opal-bright shine,
And we, gasping, beheld

A great Moonvine of pearl
Burgeon under our eyes.
And we saw it arise,
And we saw it uncurl,

An ivory fret,
A glittering stair
Of cold crystal and air,
And the end was not yet.

The brown women's tune
Chanted deeper and deeper.
We saw the pearl creeper
Lay hold of the Moon!

Then the wild song was ended
And we held our breath.
And, in silence like death,
The White Moon descended.

And first she was far
As Heaven is far.
And then she was far
As mortal things are.

And first she was round
And then ghostly with pearl,
And then she was a girl
And stepped to the ground.

She was milk of the pearl.
She was naked as light.
She was fire in the night,
White fire of the pearl.
And—she was a girl.

4

Then the women, light-drowned,
Knelt, covering their eyes,
And the radiant skies
Gave a clear, silver sound.

When someone—not I—
No—not I—but some other—
I swear it! O Mother
Of Mercies, not I!

Came crawling the track
Of an Indian asp
With a gun in his clasp
Behind her white back.

There was sand in the pan,
And the priming was damp.
And she burned like a lamp.
But he was a man.

Like hoarfrost she shined,
Like new sails in the sun,
But he raised the clubbed gun
And struck—from behind.
And then we were blind.

5

There was not a sound.
There was not a spark.
But we lay on the ground
Like bones in the dark.

In a darkness more black
Than ebony-stone,
We lay there alone
And felt our hearts crack.

Till the dawn rose in blood
And we rose without speech,
And we saw that the beach
Was the color of blood.

And we got to our boat
Without speech, and gave way
For the ship, where she lay
Like a dead man afloat.

And we got the sails set
And went out with the wind.
And the isle fell behind
But we could not forget.

How could we forget,
When we lay down to rest,
And Night bared her black breast,
And no moon rose or set?

The night came too soon.
We could live, in the sun:
But it sank and was done,
And there was not a moon.
There was never a moon.

Only darkness, clay-cold
As a snake, sucking strength—
When you caught us at length
We were madmen grown old.

But my madness is gone,
And I know where I've been.
I know what I've seen,
And I know when I'm done.

Tell Kidd to move over
His brimstone-and-rum,
For we'll be the clover
Of Hell when we come.

You hangman of tailors,
Here's Satan's doubloon!
Silk rope for the sailors
That murdered the Moon!

II CHARIOTS AND HORSEMEN

THE FIRST VISION OF HELEN

ARGUMENT—*Itys, nurtured by centaurs, meets and falls in love with Helen of Troy, before her marriage with Menelaus. What befell therefrom.*

SLOWLY blanch-handed Dawn, eyes half-awake,
Upraised magnificent the silver urn,
Heaped with white roses at the trembling lip,
Flowers that burn with crystalline accord
And die not ever. Like a pulsing heart
Beat from within against the fire-loud verge
A milky vast transparency of light
Heavy with drowning stars; a swimming void   *Morning.*
Of august ether, formless as the cloud,
And light made absolute. The mountains sighed,
Turning in sleep. Dawn held the frozen flame
An instant high above the shaggy world,
Then, to the crowing of a thousand cocks,
Poured out on earth the unconquerable sun!

The centaurs awoke! they aroused from their beds of pine,
Their long flanks hoary with dew, and their eyes, deep-
    drowned

[35]

In the primal slumber of stones, stirred bright to the shine!
And they stamped with their hooves and their gallop
    abased the ground!

The
Running
of the
Centaurs. Swifter than arrowy birds in an eager sky,
White-browed kings of the hills where old Titans feast,
—Cheiron ordered the charge with a neighing cry,
And the thousand hunters tramped like a single beast!

Beautiful monstrous dreams they seemed as they ran,
Trees come alive at the nod of a god grown mute,
Their eyes looked up to the sun like a valiant man;
Their bows clashed shrill on the loins and limbs of the
    brute,

Laughing, rejoicing, white as a naked birch,
Slim as a spear in a torrent of moving towers,
Itys, the prince, ran gay in the storm of their search,
Silverly shod on feet that outstripped the Hours!

Over by Sparta bays a horn!
Ohé, Helena!
Over by Sparta bays a horn!
And the black hound grins to his milk-teeth torn;
And the tall stag wishes he'd never been born!
Helena hunts on the hills!

Past the Eurotas the chase sweeps hot!
Ohé, Helena!
Past the Eurotas the chase sweeps hot!
And the pack has nosed at a royal slot!
And a white-armed girl has a magic lot!
Helena hunts on the hills!

[36]

Echoed at Elis the dogs give tongue!
Ohé, Helena!
Echoed at Elis the dogs give tongue!
The stag flees on but his mort is sung,
And the world and Helen are very young!
Helena hunts on the hills!

*The
Hunting
of Helen.*

Down by Argos the flight is stayed!
Ohé, Helena!
Down by Argos the flight is stayed!
And proud blood stifles the reeking blade,
And they cut the tongue for the golden maid!
Helena hunts on the hills!

Over in Troy by a kingly door,
Ohé, Helena!
Over in Troy by a kingly door,
Hector's sword is asleep from war.
"Wait!" whines the bitter steel. "Two years
    more!"
Helena hunts on the hills!

So the two molten clamors fused a space
As silver marries brass to make a bell,
Then thrust apart and vanished, save for some
Faint interlocking tentacles of sound
That chimed to Itys. Something halted him
From the swift gallop and the embracing air,
Put in him troubling languor, drove him out
To rest beside a round coin of a pool,
Casually flung among a cloud of pines.
He dreamed as a dog dreams, uneasily.

[37]

The dreams blow North and South.
Pitiless-bright they gleam.
Send, Zeus, a flower across my mouth,
The wing of a silver dream!

Itys
Dreams.

The visions smoke from the deep,
Bannering East and West.
Guide, Zeus, the stumbling old feet of Sleep,
That bring a dream to my breast!

I have gazed in immaculate eyes!
My soul is a flame astream!
Zeus, strike swift from the raging skies,
That I may die with my dream!

He woke and saw two hounds, tugging their leash,
Burst through the covert, and heard laughter bell
Like a clear stream as Helen followed them.

Itys
Beholds
Helen.

They drank, were quiet. Itys stood at gaze;
Seeing in all things one miraculous face,
And how her tunic left one bright breast bare,
And how she smoothed her hair back with one hand. . . .
But very presently he was aware
That someone not himself possessed his voice
And used it now to talk with—babbling words
Foolish and laughable to that still Beauty.

Tempest from the valiant sky,
Music of the shaken reed,
Can a thousand kisses buy
You and April, mine indeed?
Fling the dice and let them lie!

[38]

Not a joy from all your mind
Will you toss me, beggar's dole,
And you never would be kind
Though I kissed your very soul.
Race the coursers up the wind!

Itys'
Song.

Queen of desperate alarms,
Though Destruction be the priest
That must bring me to your arms,
He shall wed our bones at least!
Life was vintage, borage-crowned,
Pour the cup upon the ground!

Vines grow in my garden;
Blossoms a snake in size.
Sun warms and knife-winds harden,
Till the silk-stained globes arise;
And men peer over the hedges
With fury come in their eyes.

Pears grow in my garden;
Honey a wild bee clips.
Robbers afraid of pardon,
The princes steal from their ships,
And pluck the fruit of iniquity
And take it not from their lips.

Helen's
Song.

Fate grows in my garden;
Black as a cypress shoot.
Sleepily smiles the warden,
Guarding the gorgeous loot,
Seeing the Tree, Deliciousness,
And the tall lords dead at its root.

[39]

Their lips broke from the kiss. Helena sighed,
Then started up, afraid. Straight toward the pool
Rending the brake with hounds, shouting aloud,

The Death
of Itys.
Crashed like a cast spear the returning chase.
"Itys!" she said. "My brothers. They will kill."
He looked down at his hands that held no sword.
Helena's hounds belled answer to their pack.
Swift as a closing hand, unreal as dream,
Danger shut down around them.
                                    "Dear" he said.
Pollux, the shining-speared, burst through the leaves.

After the slaying, wide-eyed Helen paused
To clasp the dead hands loosely, and unhook
A swaying badge of gold from the white neck
That it might burn, a sun, between her breasts.
—The chase passed with hot noon, and in the cool
A straying centaur came, snuffed the new blood,
And, seeing Itys dead, neighed in loud fear;
Calling the hairy tramplers of the woods
To mourn their friend with strange solemnities.

Death-
Chant of
the
Centaurs.
Close his eyes with the coins; bind his chin with the
        shroud;
Carry this clay along, in the time of the westing cloud.
Lay you the cakes beside, for the three-mouthed dog of
        Hell;
Slain on the grass in fight, surely his end is well.

Love was the wind he sought, ignorant whence it went;
Now he has clasped it close, silent and eloquent;
Slow as the stream and strong, answering knee to knee,
Carry this clay along—it is more wise than we.

[40]

The chanting died away upon the hills,
Sobbingly low.

     And Night reversed the urn; *Night.*
Drawing all sunlight back to the hot deeps,
And leaving the high heavens full of stars.

THE LAST VISION OF HELEN

ARGUMENT—*Helen, after the fall of Troy, departs
to Egypt with ghostly companions, as in the old
tale. She encounters the Sphinx and a
marvel is wrought upon her.*

MEASURELESS sand . . . interminable sand . . .

The smooth hide of that yellow lion, Earth,
Ruffled a little and was dark again
Beneath the descending torrents of the night,
Plunging like cobalt from the cliffs of the sky,
Blotting the stiff wedge of each pyramid
With the slow gurgle of a rising wave,
A wave burning with stars. . . .
                              The Sphinx alone
Couched on her forepaws like a sleepy hound
Under the weight of a caress of rock
And smiled her woman's and chimera's smile
Inexorably, drowned with the savage dark.

The black tide filled the heavens up and ceased,
A little tonguing flame ran on the sand
Bright as a fire of paper, swift and light

As a bird's restless eyes. It rose. It bloomed,
An angry dream before the Sphinx's feet,
The exhalation of a furious thought,
Tall as the ghosts of Heaven's battlements,
The apparition that had once been Troy!

A girl went out in the summer skies,
(*The dice lie white for the throwing!*)
A girl went out in the summer skies
And the sunlight laughed as it kissed her eyes!
(*And the wind of Fate is blowing!*)

*Song of
the City
Troy.*

She was ruddy and gold as a changing leaf
When gilded Autumn gathers the sheaf.

She was lily and pale as a sleeping moth
When the full moon bleaches the skies like cloth.

The grass was glad to be under her shoe,
The poppy proud to be floor unto
The silvering dance of her feet like dew!

. . . But her lord walks chill as a cloud of snow
Where the kings of the earth are bending the bow.

They are roaring the fame of the flying dart,
But he whispers low, in a place apart,
With the evil ice of his freezing heart.

"Helena, Helena, mouth of wine,
Two more days for your sun to shine!

[43]

Helena, Helena, mouth of musk,
Two more days and I make you dusk.

Two more nights on your silky bed,
And your lover over it, bloody and dead,
And your body broken as I break bread!"

His lips are writhing, sucking and cold,
His hands are twitching like trees grown old,
He shivers as if he had trod on mold.

The *Golden Queen* at her anchor strains.
(*Sails on the sapphire, snowing.*)
Paris walks on the deck like a man in chains.
(*And the wind of Fate is blowing.*)

He wastes in his love like leaves in a flame,
But his mind is a spear in a dauntless game,
And the face of his doom has a girl's soft name.

The fifty sailors are whetting their swords.
The brown sun beats on the tarry boards.

And Helena skims by the rolling sand
And waves with the fleck of a foam-white hand.

And the blood of Youth pounds hot in the throat
As the long oars lash from the lunging boat.

Richly she came through the leaping green,
Like the shrine of a god, like a sun first seen,
And they cried, "Hurrah for the Golden Queen!"

[44]

The white sails soar like a rising gull,
The water spins by the speeding hull.

She smiles with her chin cupped into her hand
At the drowning shadow of fading land
—And Paris shakes like a torching brand.

And Paris crushes her, breath to breath,
And she gives him her honey of love and death.

But chill Menelaus a Fury hath,
He has thawed his hate to a roaring wrath!
He is loosing his hounds on the ocean-path!

The blooms of the years are withered and fall.
(*Dawn—and a red flame crowing.*)
And Time's cracked fingers number them all.
(*And the wind of Fate is blowing.*)

And a wooden horse is trampling Troy
As a hoof-thrust crushes a crumpled toy.

Ruddy and gold where the torches stare
Helena sits in her carven chair.

Lovely and strange as a moonlit cloud—
But her head droops down like a petal bowed.

Beneath her the blood and the wine run deep
—But her eyes are seas more quiet than sleep.

The drunkards brawl and the cup goes round;
But she gives no sign and she makes no sound.

Red Menelaus has poured her drink;
And she does not sip and she does not shrink.

And her mouth is a flower that says, "Depart!"
And the hilt of a knife is under her heart.

The kings of the world have finished their chase,
They dash their wine in the glorious face.

And Paris is dead in a sickly land;
And they wrench the rings from the plume-white
  hand.

They dice for her rings and the game is sweet
And lean Menelaus is smiling sleet.

And the captains chuckle, counting their scars,
For the hosts of the earth have finished their wars
And Helen and Troy are cold as the stars.

Waves in the dusk with a sound like tears
(*And the deep tide foaming and flowing.*)
Saying one name for a thousand years!
(*And the wind of Fate is blowing!*)

Like air beaten by swords, like the long cry
Of an old trumpet harsh with rust and gold,
The ballad rose assaulting, struck and died
Into a clamorous echo.   The Sphinx stirred,
Shaking the drifted moonlight from her coat
As a dog shakes water, rising mountainously;
Then from that drum of terrible stone, her throat,
Rolled back her answer at the enormous sky.

The arrow of Eros flies
In the dark, in the trembling dark;
Piercing and sweet is the song it cries
And the cup of the heart its mark!
And the cup of the heart is dust,
And the wine of the heart is spilled.
And the barb flings whimpering back to Lust
With "Master, see—I have killed!"
It was thus and thus that you were begot!
I am Death's bright arrow! Forgive me not!

The ribbon of Fate unreels
In the road of the days and nights;
There are flute-voiced airs for the dancing heels,
But over them hang the kites!
And the path grows dark as the laws
And the kites drop down in a ring,
Till a blind stag torn by the slashing claws
Is the end of the trumpeting!
It is there and there that your fathers rot!
I am Destiny's halter! Unloose me not!

The mirror of Wisdom shines
Like a face in a troubled pool.
Like the eyes of a snake are its weaving signs
To the eyes of the anxious fool.
For the secret form of the soul
Is there in its terror shown
—And it rends the sight like a burning coal
Till the eyes of the fool are stone!
It was this and this that your ardor sought!
I am Wisdom's mirror! Behold me not!

[47]

Then, like a forgotten tumult of the heart,
The multitude of men who died for Helen,
Vague, terrible, wounded forms began to chant.

Glance at us once from your sacred tower,
Helen divine!
The cutworm crawls in the almond-flower,
The rats are eating the thrones of power,
Yet glance at us once and the clouds will shower
Our lips with wine!

Loosen your hair to the storm again,
To the whistling brine!
We are very desperate men,
Reeds when fire goes over the fen,
Lighten our dark with your marvel then,
Helen divine!

Give us drink for our bitter thirst,
Helen divine!
Bless you the thieves that each priest has cursed,
Queen of us, queen of us, last and first,
Flame we followed and child we nursed,
Star at trine!

Open the heaven of your embrace,
O burning sign!
This is the end of the bloody race,
Whispering sea and the stars like lace,
You gather our souls to your shining place,
Helen divine!

[48]

The thunder ebbed away into a sigh,
Died into sand, was calm.

                              And suddenly
Helen of anguish, Helen of the song,
Helen the victory on the lips of Zeus,
Helen the princely word, the proud despair,
The voiceless cry of the ecstatic dream,
Shone with the radiance of a consuming wish
Upon the desert, and stretched out her arms
As if to take that whole great ghost of Troy,
Pennon and panoply, champion and car,
Back to its home, her breast.

Would there ever be a bud   *Helen's*
If the sap considered storm?   *Song.*
It would stay in happy mud,
Damned and sleepy, safe and warm.
Who would want to be a rose
If its petals thought of snows?

Why I lived I never knew.
Life—I took it like a toy,
Something like a worship, too,
To adore and to enjoy.
Then the gods began to play
—And the toy was put away.

Like a perfume made intense,
Like the planet of a dark,
I became magnificence
For my hour, in my spark.
There is rapture in my ghost,
Telling all my least and most.

[49]

Fate and Wisdom, judging loud,
These are shadows I can mock
With the thoughtlessness of cloud,
With the indolence of rock.
Let them air the inn they keep!
I am tired. I would sleep.

So, with the pause, all earth and sky were still
As if they had just been made—and the Sphinx lay
Silent, engulfed in silence.
                              Then she moved
Uneasily, and settled back again,
And in a low harshness of diminished sound
Spoke out her final judgment.

Zeus of the silver dawning took the scarf of a cloud,
He quickened the wraith with fire till the life cried out
    aloud,
He called Desire from his lightning, Despair from her
    weaving old,
And they fashioned the shape to a woman that men might
    die to behold!

*The
Last Song
of the
Sphinx.*

Golden Zeus of the sunbeam slapped his hand on his thigh
As the swords ran out of their scabbards and the arrows
    sang in the sky,
And the woman like leafy April was the chant that an
    archer sings
Over sands grown bloody with purple that has come from
    the hearts of kings.

Zeus of the brazen twilight, nodding his eyes awake,
Armed him a doom for Helen lest Earth burn up for her
    sake;

Chill on the heart of incense, the hands that desired so
    much,
Fell the snow-like veil of his wisdom, till the flesh was still
    at its touch.

Iron Zeus of the night-time, watching the chariot moon
Trample the skies to whiteness, turns like a moving dune
To gaze at the shade of Helen. His eyes as the skies are
    vast;
Seeing her sleep like a swallow in Death's wide bed at last.

                              Helen stood
        Within the tremendous circle of the paws,
        Moving like light towards the dark secret heart.
        The Sphinx cried terribly with a wordless sound
        Of birth and anguish struggling to be heard . . .
        And the light vanished . . .
                              And Helen and the Sphinx
        Were one forever, stone and ghost and dream—
        And Troy was gone like vapor in the dark.

So the dawn came, and toiling caravans,
Whose princes halted, arrogant as hawks,
To stare but once into the Sphinx's eyes
. . . And so were staring till Death breathed on them
With the slant feathers of his ruffling wing,
Seeking within the rock, the stubborn rock,
The gaze and burning of their Lost Desire.

WINGED MAN

THE moon, a sweeping scimitar, dipped in the stormy
    straits,
The dawn, a crimson cataract, burst through the eastern
    gates,
The cliffs were robed in scarlet, the sands were cinnabar,
Where first two men spread wings for flight and dared
    the hawk afar.

There stands the cunning workman, the crafty past all
    praise,
The man who chained the Minotaur, the man who built
    the Maze.
His young son is beside him and the boy's face is a light,
A light of dawn and wonder and of valor infinite.

Their great vans beat the cloven air, like eagles they
    mount up,
Motes in the wine of morning, specks in a crystal cup,

And lest his wings should melt apace old Dædalus flies
  low,
But Icarus beats up, beats up, he goes where lightnings go.

He cares no more for warnings, he rushes through the sky,
Braving the crags of ether, daring the gods on high,
Black 'gainst the crimson sunrise, golden o'er cloudy
  snows,
With all Adventure in his heart the first winged man
  arose.

Dropping gold, dropping gold, where the mists of morning
  rolled,
On he kept his way undaunted, though his breaths were
  stabs of cold,
Through the mystery of dawning that no mortal may
  behold.

Now he shouts, now he sings in the rapture of his wings,
And his great heart burns intenser with the strength of
  his desire,
As he circles like a swallow, wheeling, flaming, gyre on
  gyre.

Gazing straight at the sun, half his pilgrimage is done,
And he staggers for a moment, hurries on, reels back-
  ward, swerves
In a rain of scattered feathers as he falls in broken curves.

Icarus, Icarus, though the end is piteous,
Yet forever, yea, forever we shall see thee rising thus,
See the first supernal glory, not the ruin hideous.

You were Man, you who ran farther than our eyes can
    scan,
Man absurd, gigantic, eager for impossible Romance,
Overthrowing all Hell's legions with one warped and
    broken lance.

On the highest steeps of Space he will have his dwelling-
    place,
In those far, terrific regions where the cold comes down
    like Death
Gleams the red glint of his pinions, smokes the vapor of
    his breath.

Floating downward, very clear, still the echoes reach the
    ear
Of a little tune he whistles and a little song he sings,
Mounting, mounting still, triumphant, on his torn and
    broken wings!

THE RETORT DISCOURTEOUS

(*Italy—16th Century*)

BUT what, by the fur on your satin sleeves,
The rain that drags at my feather
And the great Mercurius, god of thieves,
Are we thieves doing together?

Last night your blades bit deep for their hire,
And we were the sickled barley.
To-night, atoast by the common fire,
You ask me to join your parley.

Your spears are shining like Iceland spar,
The blood-grapes drip for your drinking;
For you folk follow the rising star,
I follow the star that's sinking!

My queen is old as the frosted whins,
Nay, how could her wrinkles charm me?
And the starving bones are bursting the skins
In the ranks of her ancient army.

You marshal a steel-and-silken troop,
Your cressets are fed with spices,
And you batter the world like a rolling hoop
To the goal of your proud devices.

I have rocked your thrones—but your fight is won.
To-night, as the highest bidder,
You offer a share of your brigand-sun,
Consider, old bull, consider!

Ahead, red Death and the Fear of Death,
Your vultures, stoop to the slaughter.
But I shall fight you, body and breath,
Till my life runs out like water!

My queen is wan as the Polar snows.
Her host is a rout of specters.
But I gave her Youth like a burning rose,
And her age shall not lack protectors!

I would not turn for the thunderclap
Or the face of the woman who bore me,
With her battered badge still scarring my cap,
And the drums of defeat before me.

Roll your hands in the honey of life,
Kneel to your white-necked strumpets!
You came to your crowns with a squealing fife
But I shall go out with trumpets!

Poison the steel of the plunging dart,
Holloa your hounds to their station!
I march to my ruin with such a heart
As a king to his coronation.

Your poets roar of your golden feats—
I have herded the stars like cattle.
And you may die in the perfumed sheets,
But I shall die in battle.

ALEXANDER VI DINES
WITH THE CARDINAL OF CAPUA

NEXT, then, the peacock, gilt
With all its feathers. Look, what gorgeous dyes
Flow in the eyes!
And how deep, lustrous greens are splashed and spilt
Along the back, that like a sea-wave's crest
Scatters soft beauty o'er th' emblazoned breast!

A strange fowl! But most fit
For feasts like this, whereby I honor one
Pure as the sun!
Yet glowing with the fiery zeal of it!
Some wine? Your goblet's empty? Let it foam!
It is not often that you come to Rome.

You like the Venice glass?
Rippled with lines that float like women's curls,
Neck like a girl's,
Fierce-glowing as a chalice in the Mass?

[58]

You start—'twas artist then, not Pope who spoke!
Ave Maria stella!—ah, it broke!

'Tis said they break alone
When poison writhes within. A foolish tale!
What, you look pale?
Caraffa, fetch a silver cup! . . . You own
A Birth of Venus, now—or so I've heard,
Lovely as the breast-plumage of a bird.

Also a Dancing Faun,
Hewn with the lithe grace of Praxiteles;
Globed pearls to please
A sultan; golden veils that drop like lawn—
How happy I could be with but a tithe
Of your possessions, fortunate one! Don't writhe

But take these cushions here!
Now for the fruit! Great peaches, satin-skinned,
Rough tamarind,
Pomegranates red as lips—oh they come dear!
But men like you we feast at any price—
A plum perhaps? They're looking rather nice.

I'll cut the thing in half.
There's yours! Now, with a one-side-poisoned knife
One might snuff life
And leave one's friend with—"fool" for epitaph.
An old trick? Truth! But when one has the itch
For pretty things and isn't very rich. . . .

[59]

There, eat it all or I'll
Be angry! You feel giddy? Well, it's hot!
This bergamot
Take home and smell—it purges blood of bile;
And when you kiss Bianca's dimpled knee,
Think of the poor Pope in his misery!

Now you may kiss my ring.
Ho there, the Cardinal's litter!—You must dine
When the new wine
Is in, again with me—hear Bice sing,
Even admire my frescoes—though they're nought
Beside the calm Greek glories you have bought.

Godspeed, Sir Cardinal,
And take a weak man's blessing! Help him there
To the cool air! . . .
Lucrezia here? You're ready for the ball?
—He'll die within ten hours, I suppose—
MhM! Kiss your poor old father, little rose!

THREE DAYS' RIDE

"From Belton Castle to Solway side,
Hard by the bridge, is three days' ride."

We had fled full fast from her father's keep,
And the time was come that we must sleep.

The first day was an ecstasy,
A golden mist, a burgeoning tree;
We rode like gods through a world new-made,
The hawthorn scented hill and glade,
A faint, still sweetness in the air—
And, oh, her face and the wind in her hair!
And the steady beat of our good steeds' hooves,
Bearing us northward, strong and fast,
To my high black tower, stark to the blast,
Like a swimmer stripped where the Solway moves.

[61]

And ever, riding, we chanted a song,
Challenging Fortune, loud and long,
"From Belton Castle to Solway side,
Strive as you may, is three days' ride!"

She slept for an hour, wrapped in my cloak,
And I watched her till the morning broke;
The second day—and a harsher land,
And grey bare hills on either hand;
A surly land and a sullen folk,
And a fog that came like bitter smoke.

The road wound on like a twisted snake,
And our horses sobbed as they topped the brake.
Till we sprang to earth at Wyvern Fen,
Where fresh steeds stamped, and were off again.
Weary and sleepless, bruised and worn,
We still had strength for laughter and scorn;
Love held us up through the mire and mist,
Love fed us, while we clasped and kissed,
And still we sang as the night closed in,
Stealthy and slow as a hidden sin,
"From Belton Castle to Solway side,
Ride how you will, is three days' ride."

My love drooped low on the black mare's back,
Drowned in her hair . . . the reins went slack . . .
Yet she could not sleep, save to dream bad dreams
And wake all trembling, till at last
Her golden head lay on my breast.

At last we saw the first faint gleams
Of day. Dawn broke. A sickly light
Came from the withered sun—a blight

[62]

Was on the land, and poisonous mist
Shrouded the rotting trees, unkissed
By any wind, and black crags glared
Like sightless, awful faces, spared
From death to live accursed for aye.

Dragging slow chains the hours went by.
We rode on, drunk and drugged with sleep,
Too deadly weary now to say
Whether our horses kept the way
Or no—like slaves stretched on a heap
Of poisoned arrows. Every limb
Shot with sharp pain; pain seemed to swim
Like a red cloud before our eyes. . . .

The mist broke, and a moment showed,
Sharp as the Devil's oxen-goad,
The spear-points where the hot chase rode.

Idly I watched them dance and rise
Till white wreaths wiped them out again . . .
My love jerked at the bridle rein;
The black mare, dying, broke her heart
In one swift gallop; for my part
I dozed; and ever in my brain,
Four hoofs of fire beat out refrain,
A dirge to light us down to death,
A silly rhyme that saith and saith,
"From Belton Castle to Solway side,
Though great hearts break, is three days' ride!"
The black mare staggered, reeled and fell,
Bearing my love down . . . a great bell
Began to toll . . . and sudden fire
Flared at me from the road, a pyre

It seemed, to burn our bodies in . . .
And I fell down, far down, within
The pit's mouth . . . and my brain went blind. . . .

I woke—a cold sun rose behind
Black evil hills—my love knelt near
Beside a stream, her golden hair
Streaming across the grass—below
The Solway eddied to and fro,
White with fierce whirlpools . . . my love turned. . . .
Thank God, some hours of joy are burned
Into the mind, and will remain,
Fierce-blazing still, in spite of pain!

They came behind us as we kissed,
Stealthily from the dripping mist,
Her brothers and their evil band.
They bound me fast and made me stand.
They forced her down upon her knees.
She did not strive or cry or call,
But knelt there dumb before them all—
I could not turn away my eyes—
There was no fear upon her face,
Although they slew her in that place.
The daggers rent and tore her breast
Like dogs that snarl above a kill,
Her proud face gazed above them still,
Seeking rest—Oh, seeking rest!
The blood swept like a crimson dress
Over her bosom's nakedness,
A curtain for her weary eyes,
A muffling-cloth to stop her sighs . . .
And she was gone—and a red thing lay
Silent, on the trampled clay.

Beneath my horse my feet are bound,
My hands are bound behind my back,
I feel the sinews start and crack—
And ever to the hoof-beats' sound,
As we draw near the gallows-tree,
Where I shall hang right speedily,
A crazy tune rings in my brain,
Four hoofs of fire tramp the refrain,
Crashing clear o'er the roaring crowd,
Steadily galloping, strong and loud,
"From Belton Castle to Solway side,
Hard by the bridge, is three days' ride!"

CAROL: NEW STYLE

If Jesus Christ *should come again,*
On Christmas day, on Christmas day,
To bother the minds of gentlemen
On Christmas day in the morning?

The first one said as he passed by,
As he passed by, as he passed by,
"I see three thieves a-hanging high,
This Christmas day in the morning."

The second one said, "What sinful men!
What sinful men, what sinful men!
Hanging is too good for them,
On Christmas day in the morning."

The third one said, "Oh stay your word!
Stay your word, oh stay your word!
Do you not see that one's the Lord,
This Christmas day in the morning?"

"I know him by his weary head,
His weary head, his weary head."
Whereat they all fell sore adread,
That Christmas day in the morning.

"How sad this is we all avow,
Yes indeed, we all avow!
But what shall we do about it now,
On Christmas day in the morning?"

PRIMUS

"I'll run away as fast as I may,
As fast as I may, as fast as I may,
And pretend I haven't been out all day,
On Christmas day in the morning."

SECUNDUS

"I'll buy Him a shroud that's spick and span,
Spick and span, spick and span,
For I was always a generous man,
On Christmas day in the morning."

TERTIUS

"But what if we should cut Him down,
Cut Him down, cut Him down?"

SECUNDUS ET PRIMUS

"You fool, do you want to arouse the town,
On Christmas day in the morning?"

"My speech was rash," the third one said,
The third one said, the third one said.
"We're surer of God when we know He's dead,
On any day in the morning."

They knelt in the snow and prayed and bowed,
Prayed and bowed, prayed and bowed,
And the two dead thieves laughed out aloud
On Christmas day in the morning.

As Jesus Christ was hanging high,
Hanging high, hanging high,
He saw three Christians, passing by,
On Christmas day in the morning.

III SKYSCRAPER HOUSE

RAIN AFTER A VAUDEVILLE SHOW

The last pose flickered, failed. The screen's dead white
Glared in a sudden flooding of harsh light
Stabbing the eyes; and as I stumbled out
The curtain rose. A fat girl with a pout
And legs like hams, began to sing "His Mother."
Gusts of bad air rose in a choking smother;
Smoke, the wet steam of clothes, the stench of plush,
Powder, cheap perfume, mingled in a rush.
I stepped into the lobby—and stood still
Struck dumb by sudden beauty, body and will.
Cleanness and rapture—excellence made plain—
The storming, thrashing arrows of the rain!
Pouring and dripping on the roofs and rods,
Smelling of woods and hills and fresh-turned sods,
Black on the sidewalks, grey in the far sky,
Crashing on thirsty panes, on gutters dry,
Hurrying the crowd to shelter, making fair
The streets, the houses, and the heat-soaked air,—
Merciful, holy, charging, sweeping, flashing,

It smote the soul with a most iron clashing! . . .
Like dragons' eyes the street-lamps suddenly gleamed,
Yellow and round and dim, low globes of flame.
And, scarce-perceived, the clouds' tall banners streamed.
Out of the petty wars, the daily shame,
Beauty strove suddenly, and rose, and flowered. . . .
I gripped my coat and plunged where awnings lowered.
Made one with hissing blackness, caught, embraced,
By splendor and by striving and swift haste—
Spring coming in with thunderings and strife—
I stamped the ground in the strong joy of life!

LUNCH–TIME ALONG BROADWAY

Twelve-thirty bells from a thousand clocks, the type-
    writer tacks and stops,
Gorged elevators slam and fall through the floors like
    water-drops,
From offices hung like sea-gulls' nests on a cliff the whirl-
    winds beat,
The octopus-crowd comes rolling out, his tentacles crawl
    for meat.

He snuffles his way by restaurants where lily-voiced
    women feast,
He pokes his muzzle through white-tiled caves, and gulps
    like a hungry beast,
He roots into subterranean holes, he sweeps hell's tables
    bare,
His suckers settle and fix and drink like wasps on a burst-
    ing pear.

The wildcat quarrel of traffic soothes to a smooth rolling
of tires
And the waterflow sound of the feeding brute as he pads
by the cooking-fires,
His body shoulders the canyoned streets, his gluttonous
mouths expand
And he laps the fat and flesh of the earth as a cat laps milk
from a hand.

Slowly the greedy claws curl back, the feelers recoil and
close,
The flood is setting the other way with the avalanche
pound of snows,
Heavy and hot as a sated bee, enormous, slower than oil,
The beast comes shuffling to lair again, his lips still wet
with his spoil.

THE WALKERS

(Strike Pickets—Lower Fifth Ave.)

IT IS past day and its brilliance, it is not yet sumptuous
    night
For the moon to shine on gardened roofs like a white nut
    peeled of its husk,
The march of the ant-hill crowds below is like sand falling
    from a height,
And the lost horns of the taxis cry hooting through the
    dusk.

Grey as rain in an autumn wood when the skies are pale
    with cloud
Are the light and the street and the faces where the
    elephant busses roll,
Dark motors shine like a seal's wet skin, and they and their
    rich are proud,
But the walkers are dim and aimless on a dolorous way of
    the soul.

I watch, and my soft, pleased body cries for the rooms with
  lights like flowers,
For the delicate talk of women, and music's deep-perfumed
  smart,
And I sweat at the walkers crushed by machining, implacable hours,
And in torment I turn away—but their march is over my
  heart.

They are helpless as drifting weed, they are stung with
  insane impatience
At themselves and their lords and their hunger no toil can
  feed till it sleeps.
They are racked earth hating the plow, they are dung at
  the roots of the nations,
They are wheat that will not be bread and burns at the
  scythe that reaps.

Ensigns of honor they bear not, their songs are ignorant
  clamors.
I hate their joy and their fear. I am bitter afraid of pain.
But the pitiful tune of their feet is trampling my soul with
  hammers,
And I must follow them out in the desolate face of the rain.

Ask not watchword nor sign—there is neither tocsin nor
  clarion;
Only the strength of the flood, the might of the falling
  snow,
The cry of the bitter clay to the God who devised it carrion,
The purblind silence of sleep, as night to the night we flow.

8:30 A.M. ON 32ND STREET

THE *wind sniffed like a happy cat*
At scuttling beetle-people,
The sunshine would have roused a flat
To try and be a steeple.

My breakfast in me warm and staunch,
Your letter in my pocket,
The world's a coon that's climbed a branch
And I am David Crockett.

Time hoards our lives with griping care
And barren is his bursary,
But he'll make diamonds of the air
Upon one anniversary!

Five years ago I saw you first
And knew in every part
The flagrant and immortal thirst
Love salts into the heart.

[77]

Five years ago the Pleiad crew
Sang in their starry hive,
Because a miracle like you
Could dare to be alive.

Five years, and still, through earth's degrees
You, like a pageant, pass;
Courageous as invading seas
And careless as the grass.

Pauper poets of rimes grown thin
Mutter their madhouse wrongs.
I have aeons to love you in,
Ages to make you songs!

Pour your rain on the bitter tree!
Harrow the soil with spears!
I shall grow you Felicity,
After a million years!

The street-signs winked like smiles at me,
The wind pawed by enchanted;
The sun swung high for all to see.
I'd stop him if I wanted!

HYMN IN COLUMBUS CIRCLE

(After Seeing a Certain Window Display)

MAN in his secret shrine
Hallows a wealth of gods,
Black little basalt Baals
Wood-kings heard in the pine,
Josses whose jade prevails
Breaking Disaster's rods;
Prayers have made each one shine.

Man's is a pious race.
Once he knelt to the moss,
Ra, Astarte or Jove,
Deities great and base,
—Once his questionings clove
To the stubborn arms of the Cross
That smote all lies in the face.

Here is a new desire,
One of his latest lauds
Throned on marble and praised
With the lovely softness of fire.
Signs acclaim it amazed,
Its window-altar is hazed,
And every gazer applauds
The tremendous rubber tire.

IV KING DAVID

KING DAVID

DAVID sang to his hook-nosed harp:
"The Lord God is a jealous God!
His violent vengeance is swift and sharp!
And the Lord is King above all gods!

"Blest be the Lord, through years untold,
The Lord Who has blessed me a thousand fold!

"Cattle and concubines, corn and hives
Enough to last me a dozen lives.

"Plump, good women with noses flat,
Marrowful blessings, weighty and fat.

"I wax in His peace like a pious gourd,
The Lord God is a pleasant God,
Break mine enemy's jaw, O Lord!
For the Lord is King above all gods!"

His hand dropped slack from the tunable strings,
A sorrow came on him—a sorrow of kings.

A sorrow sat on the arm of his throne,
An eagle sorrow with claws of stone.

"I am merry, yes, when I am not thinking,
But life is nothing but eating and drinking.

"I can shape my psalms like daggers of jade,
But they do not shine like the first I made.

"I can harry the heathen from North to South,
But no hot taste comes into my mouth.

"My wives are comely as long-haired goats,
But I would not care if they cut their throats!

"Where are the maids of the desert tents
With lips like flagons of frankincense?

"Where is Jonathan? Where is Saul?
The captain-towers of Zion wall?

"The trees of cedar, the hills of Nod,
The kings, the running lions of God?

"Their words were a writing in golden dust,
Their names are myrrh in the mouths of the just.

"The sword of the slayer could never divide them—
Would God I had died in battle beside them!"

The Lord looked down from a thunder-clap.
(The Lord God is a crafty God.)
He heard the strings of the shrewd harp snap.
(The Lord Who is King above all gods.)

He pricked the king with an airy thorn,
It burnt in his body like grapes of scorn.

The eyelids roused that had drooped like lead.
David lifted his heavy head.

The thorn stung at him, a fiery bee,
"The world is wide. I will go and see
From the roof of my haughty palace," said he.

2

Bathsheba bathed on her vine-decked roof.
(The Lord God is a mighty God.)
Her body glittered like mail of proof.
(And the Lord is King above all gods.)

Her body shimmered, tender and white
As the flesh of aloes in candlelight.

King David forgot to be old or wise.
He spied on her bathing with sultry eyes.

A breath of spice came into his nose.
He said, "Her breasts are like two young roes."

His eyes were bright with a crafty gleam.
He thought, "Her body is soft as cream."

[85]

He straightened himself like an unbent bow
And called a servant and bade him go.

3

Uriah the Hittite came to his lord,
Dusty with war as a well-used sword.

A close, trim man like a belt, well-buckled;
A jealous gentleman, hard to cuckold.

David entreated him, soft and bland,
Offered him comfits from his own hand.

Drank with him deep till his eyes grew red,
And laughed in his beard as he went to bed.

The days slipped by without hurry or strife,
Like apple-parings under a knife,
And still Uriah kept from his wife.

Lean fear tittered through David's psalm,
"This merry husband is far too calm."

David sent for Uriah then,
They greeted each other like pious men.

"Thou hast borne the battle, the dust and the heat.
Go down to thy house and wash thy feet!"

Uriah frowned at the words of the king.
His brisk, hard voice had a leaden ring.

"While the hosts of God still camp in the field
My house to me is a garden sealed.

"How shall I rest while the arrow yet flies?
The dust of the war is still in my eyes."

David spoke with his lion's roar:
"If Peace be a bridle that rubs you sore,
You shall fill your belly with blood and war!"

Uriah departed, calling him kind.
His eyes were serpents in David's mind.

He summoned a captain, a pliable man,
"Uriah the Hittite shall lead the van.

"In the next assault, when the fight roars high,
And the Lord God is a hostile God,
Retire from Uriah that he may die.
For the Lord is King above all gods."

4

The messenger came while King David played
The friskiest ditty ever made.

"News, O King, from our dubious war!
The Lord of Hosts hath prevailed once more!

"His foes are scattered like chirping sparrows,
Their kings lie breathless, feathered with arrows.

[87]

"Many are dead of your captains tall.
Uriah the Hittite was first to fall."

David turned from the frolicsome strings
And rent his clothes for the death of kings.

Yet, as he rent them, he smiled for joy.
The sly, wide smile of a wicked boy.

"The powerful grace of the Lord prevails!
He has cracked Uriah between His nails!

"His blessings are mighty, they shall not cease.
And my days henceforth shall be days of peace!"

His mind grew tranquil, smoother than fleece.
He rubbed his body with scented grease.
And his days thenceforward were days of peace.

His days were fair as the flowering lime
—For a little time, for a little time.

And Bathsheba lay in his breast like a dove,
A vessel of amber, made for love.

5

When Bathsheba was great with child,
(The Lord God is a jealous God!)
Portly and meek as a moon grown mild,
(The Lord is King above all gods!)

Nathan, the prophet, wry and dying,
Preached to the king like a locust crying:

"Hearken awhile to a doleful thing!
There were two men in thy land, O King!

"One was rich as a gilded ram.
One had one treasure, a poor ewe-lamb.

"Rich man wasted his wealth like spittle.
Poor man shared with his lamb spare victual.

"A traveler came to the rich man's door.
'Give me to eat, for I hunger sore!'

"Rich man feasted him fatly, true,
But the meat that he gave him was fiend's meat, too,
Stolen and roasted, the poor man's ewe!

"Hearken, my lord, to a deadly thing!
What shall be done with these men, O King?"

David hearkened, seeing it plain,
His heart grew heavy with angry pain:
"Show me the rich man that he be slain!"

Nathan barked as a jackal can.
"Just, O King! And thou art the man!"

David rose as the thunders rise
When someone in Heaven is telling lies.
But his eyes were weaker than Nathan's eyes.

[89]

His huge bulk shivered like quaking sod,
Shoulders bowing to Nathan's rod,
Nathan, the bitter apple of God.

His great voice shook like a runner's, spent,
"My sin has found me! Oh, I repent!"

Answered Nathan, that talkative Jew:
"For many great services, comely and true,
The Lord of Mercy will pardon you.

"But the child in Bathsheba, come of your seed,
Shall sicken and die like a blasted weed."

David groaned when he heard him speak.
The painful tears ran hot on his cheek.

Ashes he cast on his kingly locks.
All night long he lay on the rocks.

Beseeching his Lord with a howling cry:
"O Lord God, O my jealous God,
Be kind to the child that it may not die,
For Thou art King above all gods!"

6

Seven long nights he lay there, howling,
A lion wounded, moaning and growling.

Seven long midnights, sorrowing greatly,
While Sin, like a dead man, embraced him straitly.

Till he was abased from his lust and pride
And the child was born and sickened and died.

He arose at last. It was ruddy Day.
And his sin like water had washed away.

He cleansed and anointed, took fresh apparel,
And worshiped the Lord in a tuneful carol.

His servants, bearing the child to bury,
Marveled greatly to see him so merry.

He spoke to them mildly as mid-May weather:
"The child and my sin are perished together.

"He is dead, my son. Though his whole soul yearn to me,
I must go to him, he may not return to me.

"Why should I sorrow for what was pain?
A cherished grief is an iron chain."

He took up his harp, the sage old chief.
His heart felt clean as a new green leaf.

His soul smelt pleasant as rain-wet clover.
"I have sinned and repented and that's all over.

"In his dealings with heathen, the Lord is hard.
But the humble soul is his spikenard."

His wise thoughts fluttered like doves in the air.
"I wonder is Bathsheba still so fair?

"Does she weep for the child that our sin made perish?
I must comfort my ewe-lamb, comfort and cherish.

"The justice of God is honey and balm.
I will soothe her heart with a little psalm."

He went to her chamber, no longer sad,
Walking as light as a shepherd lad.

He found her weeping, her garments rent,
Trodden like straw by God's punishment.
He solaced her out of his great content.

Being but woman, a while she grieved,
But at last she was comforted, and conceived.

Nine months later she bore him a son.
(The Lord God is a mighty God!)
The name of that child was SOLOMON.
He was God's tough staff till his days were run!
(And the Lord is King above all gods!)

V MY FAIR LADY

CHEMICAL ANALYSIS

SHE's slender hands and pretty lips,
And seafoam and rosemary.
Her ears are pointed at the tips,
She stayed so long in Fairy.

NOMENCLATURE

Some people have names like pitchforks, some people
    have names like cakes,
Names full of sizzling esses like a family quarrel of snakes,
Names black as a cat, vermilion as the cockscomb-hat
    of a fool—
But your name is a green, small garden, a rush asleep in a
    pool.

When God looked at the diffident cherubs and dropped
    them out of the sky,
He named them like Adam's animals, while Mary and
    Eve stood by,
The poor things huddled before him in scared little naked
    flocks
—And he gave you a name like sunlight, and clover, and
    hollyhocks.

For your mouth with its puzzled jesting, for your hair like
    a dark soft bird,
Shy humor and dainty walking, sweet laughter and
    subtle word,
As a fairy walks with a mushroom to keep the rain from
    its things
You carry your name forever, like a scepter alive with
    wings.

Neither change nor despair shall touch it nor the seasons
    make it uncouth,
It will burn like an Autumn maple when your proud age
    talks to your youth,
Wise child, clean friend, adoration, light arrow of God,
    white flame,
I would break my body to pieces to call you once by your
    name!

DIFFERENCE

My MIND's a map. A mad sea-captain drew it
Under a flowing moon until he knew it;
Winds with brass trumpets, puffy-cheeked as jugs,
And states bright-patterned like Arabian rugs.
"Here there be tygers." "Here we buried Jim."
Here is the strait where eyeless fishes swim
About their buried idol, drowned so cold
He weeps away his eyes in salt and gold.
A country like the dark side of the moon,
A cider-apple country, harsh and boon,
A country savage as a chestnut-rind,
A land of hungry sorcerers.

Your mind?

—Your mind is water through an April night,
A cherry-branch, plume-feathery with its white,
A lavender as fragrant as your words,
A room where Peace and Honor talk like birds,

Sewing bright coins upon the tragic cloth
Of heavy Fate, and Mockery, like a moth,
Flutters and beats about those lovely things.
You are the soul, enchanted with its wings,
The single voice that raises up the dead
To shake the pride of angels.

                                    I have said.

A SAD SONG

ROSEMARY, *Rosemary,*
There's a Pig in your garden,
With silk bristles frizzy
And tushers of snow!
But Rosemary was cautious,
She said, "Beg your pardon!
I'm really too busy
To look down below."

Rosemary, Rosemary,
There's a Bird in your kitchen!
His voice is gold water,
He says, "Pretty Poll!"
But Rosemary heard nothing,
Putting stitch after stitch in
The dress of a daughter,
Her thirty-sixth doll.

[100]

Rosemary, Rosemary,
A silver-winged Rabbit!
He bridles and gentles
And wants you astride!
"I prefer," said Rosemary,
"To ride a Good Habit."
She went buying black lentils—
She did till she died.

A NONSENSE SONG

ROSEMARY, Rosemary, let down your hair!
The cow's in the hammock, the crow's in the chair!
I was making you songs out of sawdust and silk,
But they came in to call and they spilt them like milk.

The cat's in the coffee, the wind's in the east,
He screams like a peacock and whines like a priest
And the saw of his voice makes my blood turn to mice—
So let down your long hair and shut off his advice!

Pluck out the thin hairpins and let the waves stream,
Brown-gold as brook-waters that dance through a dream,
Gentle-curled as young cloudlings, sweet-fragrant as bay,
Till it takes all the fierceness of living away.

Oh, when you are with me, my heart is white steel.
But the bat's in the belfry, the mold's in the meal,
And I think I hear skeletons climbing the stair!
—Rosemary, Rosemary, let down your bright hair!

TO ROSEMARY
ON THE METHODS BY WHICH
SHE MIGHT BECOME AN ANGEL

NOT where the sober sisters, grave as willows,
Walk like old twilights by the jasper sea,
Nor where the plump hunt of cherubs holly-hilloes
Chasing their ruddy fox, the sun, you'll be!

Not with the stained-glass prophets, bearded grimly,
Not with the fledgling saved, meek Wisdom's lot,
Kissing a silver book that glimmers dimly,
For acolytes are mild and you are not.

They'll give you a curled tuba, tall as Rumor,
They'll sit you on a puff of Autumn cloud,
Gilded-fantastic as your scorn and humor
And let you blow that tuba much too loud.

Against the unceasing chant to sinless Zion,
Three impudent seraph notes, three starry coals,
Sweet as wild grass and happy as a lion
—And all the saints will throw you aureoles.

EVENING AND MORNING

OVER the roof, like burnished men,
The stars tramp high.
You blink—the fire blinks back again
With a cock's red eye.
Lay your book away to doze,
Say your silly prayers,
See that nothing grabs your toes
And run upstairs!

Sandman eyes and heavy head,
Sleep comes soon,
Pouring on your quiet bed
The great, cool moon.
Nod's green wheel of moss turns round,
Dripping dreams and peace,
Gentle as a pigeon's sound,
Soft as fleece.

Think of warm sheep shuffling home,
Stones sunk deep,
Bees inside a honeycomb—
Sleep—Sleep.
Smile as when young Una smiled,
Hard and sweet and gay,
Bitter saint, fantastic child,
Fold your wings away.

Dawn, the owl, is fluttering
At Day's bright bars.
Night, the lame man, puttering,
Puffs out the stars.
Wake! and hear an airy shout
Crack the egg of cloud,
And see the golden bird creep out,
Ruffling and proud.

IN A GLASS
OF WATER BEFORE RETIRING

Now the day
Burns away.
Most austere
Night is here
—Time for sleep.

And, to sleep,
If you please,
For release
Into peace,
Think of these.

Snails that creep,
Silver-slow;
Streams that flow,
Murmuring,
Murmuring;

Bells that chime,
Sweet—clear—c-o-o-l;
Of a pool
Hushed so still
Stars drowse there,
Sleepy-fair;
Of a hill
Drenched with night,
Drowned with moon's
Lovely light;
Of soft tunes,
Played so slow,
Kind and low,
You sink down,
Into down,
Into rest,
Into the perfect whiteness,
The drowsy, drowsy lightness,
The warm, clean, sleepy feathers of a
    slumbering bird's white breast.

LEGEND

THE trees were sugared like wedding-cake
With a bright hoar frost, with a very cold snow,
When we went begging for Jesus' sake,
Penniless children, years ago.

Diamond weather—but nothing to eat
In that fine, bleak bubble of earth and skies.
Nothing alive in the windy street
But two young children with hungry eyes.

"We must go begging or we will die.
I would sell my soul for an apple-core!"
So we went mendicant, you and I,
Knock-knock-knock at each snow-choked door.

Knock-knock-knock till our fingers froze.
Nobody even replied, "Good day!",
Only the magistrate, toasting his toes,
Howled at us sleepily, "Go away!"

"Rosemary dear, what shall we do?"
"Stephen, I know not. Beseech some saint!
My nose has turned to an icicle blue,
And my belly within me is very faint."

"If there be saints, they are fast asleep,
Lounging in Heaven, in wraps of feather."
"Talk not so, or my eyes will weep
Till the ice-tears rattle and clink together."

"Saints are many—on which shall I call?
He must be kindly, without constraint."
"I think you had better pray to Saint Paul.
I have heard people call him a neighborly saint."

Down he flopped on his cold, bare knees
—Breath that smoked in the bitter air—
Crossing his body with hands afreeze,
He sought Saint Paul in a vehement prayer.

Scarce had these shiverers piped, "Amen,"
Cheeping like fledglings, crying for bread,
When good Saint Paul appeared to them then,
With a wide gold halo around his head.

He waved his episcopal hand, and smiled,
And the ground was spread like a banquet-table!
"Here is much good food for each hungry child,
And I hope you will eat as long as you're able."

"Here are good, thick cloaks for your ragged backs,
And strong, warm boots for your feet," said he,
"And for Stephen, gloves and a little axe,
And a little fur muff for Rosemary."

They thanked him humbly, saying a Pater,
Before they had touched a morsel even,
But he said, "Your thanks are for One far greater"
And pointed his right arm up at Heaven.

"For you are the sparrows around God's door,
He will lift you up like His own great banner.
But the folk who made you suffer so sore—
He shall deal with them in another manner.

"It is His own will to transport those folk
To a region of infinite ice and snow."
And his breath was a taper of incense-smoke,
And he lifted a finger—and it was so.

And the folk were gone—and the saint was fled—
And we stared and stared at the wintry land.
And in front of us there was a banquet spread.
And a little fur muff on Rosemary's hand.

DULCE RIDENTEM

The bee, he has white honey,
The Sunday child her muff,
The rich man lots of money
Though never quite enough,
The apple has a Springtime smell,
The star-fields silver grain,
But I have youth, the cockleshell,
And the sweet laugh of Jane.

The lark's tune goes so clearly
But Jane's is clear wells.
The cuckoo's voice currs cheerly,
But Jane's is new bells.
Whether she chuckles like a dove,
Or laughs like April rain,
It is her heart and hands and love,
The moth-wing soul of Jane.

ALL NIGHT LONG

WE WERE in bed by nine, but she did not hear the clock,
She lay in her quiet first sleep, soft-breathing, head by her
    arm,
And the rising, radiant moon spilled silver out of its crock
On her hair and forehead and eyes as we rested, gentle and
    warm.

All night long it remained, that calm, compassionate sheet,
All the long night it wrapped us in whiteness like ermine-
    fur,
I did not sleep all the night, but lay, with wings on my feet,
Still, the cool at my lips, seeing her, worshipping her.

Oh, the bright sparks of dawn when day broke, burning
    and wild!
Oh, the first waking glance from her sleepy, beautiful eyes!
With a heart and a mind newborn as a naked, young,
    golden child,
I took her into my arms. We saw the morning arise!

DAYS PASS: MEN PASS

WHEN, like all liberal girls and boys,
We too get rid of sight
—The juggler with his painted toys
The elf and her delight—

In the cool place where jests are few
And there's no time to weep
For all the untamed hearts we knew
Creeping like moths to sleep.

This eagerness that burns us yet
Will rot like summer snow,
And we'll forget as winds forget
When they have ceased to blow.

Oh, we'll grow sleepy, lacking mirth!
But there will still endure
Somewhere, like innocence and earth,
The things your wish made pure.

Wide moonlight on a harvest dew,
White silk, too dear to touch,
These will be you and always you
When I am nothing much.

The flowers with the hardy eyes,
The bread that feeds the gods,
These will be you till Last Assize
When I'm improper sods.

Oh dear immortal, while you can,
Commit one mortal sin.
And let me love you like a man
Till Judgment Day comes in!

HEART'S BLOOD

OTHERS can offer you the courtly red
That lies in veins just underneath the skin
Which may be fathomed with a silver pin
That leaves no scar to show the flesh has bled.
And others still, that deep, arterial flood
Dark as wood-violets sodden in the rain.
That gift is rare but may be given again.
I have a different taste, in giving blood.

Take up the cup. It will not dye your hand
With pretty little threads of scarlet waste
Or purples that can have a counterpart.
Yet, it has virtues—for I understand
Such clotted liquor is not brewed in haste
And can be got from nowhere but the heart.

ILLA

THIS is only the shadow of what she was once;
The rest is Honor's.
Nevertheless, O Death, be humble in claiming
Even that shadow.

VI SONNETS AND PORTRAITS

THE GOLDEN CORPSE

(Eight Sonnets for Donald Malcolm Campbell)

STRIPPED country, shrunken as a beggar's heart,
Inviolate landscape, hardened into steel,
Where the cold soil shatters under heel
Day after day like armor cracked apart.

Winter Connecticut, whose air is clean
As a new icicle to cut the throat,
Whose black and rigid trees will not demean
Themselves to swagger in a crystal coat.

I hate you as a bastard hates his name
When your cramped hills are hostile with the white,
But, every year, when March comes in the same,
A frozen river rolling in the night,

I must go back and hunt among your snow
Something I lost there, much too long ago.

It was not innocence, it was not scorn,
And yet it had these names and many more.
It was a champion blowing on a horn,
It was the running of a golden boar.

It was a stallion, trampling the skies
To rags of lightning with his glittering shoes,
It was a childish god with lazy eyes,
It was an indolent and reckless Muse.

More than all these, it was a spirit apart,
Purely of fire and air and the mind.
No fear could eat the temper from its heart
Nor any fleshly bandage make it blind.

It was a silver dagger in the blast.
It was the first of youth, and it has passed.

3

I left it in a bare and windy street
Between two sets of bells whose casual chimes
Answer each other, janglingly and sweet,
Like the concord of long-repeated rhymes.

I left it in a since-demolished bar,
And underneath a rain-streaked paving-stone.
And, men and things being what they are,
The hidden ghost had better couch alone.

I shall not rattle with an iron fist
The relics, scattered into sticks of chalk,
Of what was once the carcass of a hawk
That sat like Wrath on an archangel's wrist.

Nor disinter, to make my house look smart,
That thunder-broken and ferocious heart.

4

Men that dig up a mandrake know dis-ease.
This body is committed to its bones
Down where the taproots of New England trees
Suck bare existence from the broken stones.

All summer cannot quicken it with heat,
Nor Spring perturb it with a budding bough,
Nor all the glittering devils of the sleet
In snowing Winter rack its quiet now.

But, in October, when the apples fall,
And leaves begin to rust before the cold,
There may occur, by some unnoticed wall,
A sigh, a whisper in the rotten gold.

A breath that hardly can be called a breath
From Death that will not yet acknowledge Death.

5

Unnoticed—for the years have hardier tasks
Than listening to a whisper or a sigh.
They creep among us with a bag of masks
And fit them to our brows obsequiously.

Some are of iron, to affront the gay,
And some of bronze, to satirize the brave,
But most are merely a compost of clay
Cut in the sleepy features of a slave.

With such astuteness do they counterfeit,
We do not realize the masks are on
Till, gaudy in our folly, bit by bit
We notice that a neighbor's face seems drawn.

And then, with fingers turned to lumps of stone,
Touch the inhuman cast that was our own.

6

There is no doubt such workmanship is sage.
The bound and ordered skies could not abide
A creature formed of elemental rage
For longer than a moment of its pride.

The hand that stooped to Adam from the cloud
And touched his members with a fiery spine
Designed as well the pattern of the shroud
That should convince him he was not divine.

And there are sorceries more excellent
Than the first conflagration of the dust,
But none are quite so single in intent
Or unsophisticated with distrust.

The ripened fruit is golden to the core
But an enchantment fosters it no more.

7

Therefore, in neither anguish nor relief,
I offer to the shadow in the air
No image of a monumental grief
To mock its transience from a stony chair,

Nor any tablets edged in rusty black.
Only a branch of maple, gathered high
When the crisp air first tastes of applejack,
And the blue smokes of Autumn stain the sky.

A branch whose leaves cling to the withering staff
Like precious toys of gilt and scarlet paint,
An emblem Life and Death share half-and-half,
A brittle sceptre for a dying saint.

Unburning fire, an insubstantial Host,
A violence dreamt, a beauty of the ghost.

8

So much in memory. For the future, this.
The checkerboarded house of Day and Night
Is but a cavern where a swallow flies
To beat its wings an instant at the light

And then depart, where the incessant storm
Shepherds the planets like a drunken nurse.
It does not need an everlasting form
To dignify an ecstasy so terse.

But while the swallow fluttered and was quick
I have marked down its passage in the dark
And charred its image on a broken stick
With the brief flame of an uncertain spark.

The fire can have it now, the rain can rain on it,
And the ice harden like a god's disdain on it.

PORTRAIT OF A BOY

AFTER the whipping he crawled into bed,
Accepting the harsh fact with no great weeping.
How funny uncle's hat had looked striped red!
He chuckled silently. The moon came, sweeping
A black, frayed rag of tattered cloud before
In scorning; very pure and pale she seemed,
Flooding his bed with radiance. On the floor
Fat motes danced. He sobbed, closed his eyes and dreamed.

Warm sand flowed round him. Blurts of crimson light
Splashed the white grains like blood. Past the cave's mouth
Shone with a large, fierce splendor, wildly bright,
The crooked constellations of the South;
Here the Cross swung; and there, affronting Mars,
The Centaur stormed aside a froth of stars.
Within, great casks, like wattled aldermen,
Sighed of enormous feasts, and cloth of gold
Glowed on the walls like hot desire. Again,

Beside webbed purples from some galleon's hold,
A black chest bore the skull and bones in white
Above a scrawled "Gunpowder!" By the flames,
Decked out in crimson, gemmed with syenite,
Hailing their fellows with outrageous names,
The pirates sat and diced. Their eyes were moons.
"Doubloons!" they said. The words crashed gold.
    "Doubloons!"

MUSIC

MY FRIEND went to the piano; spun the stool
A little higher; left his pipe to cool;
Picked up a fat green volume from the chest;
And propped it open.

               Whitely without rest,
His fingers swept the keys that flashed like swords,
. . . And to the brute drums of barbarian hordes,
Roaring and thunderous and weapon-bare,
An army stormed the bastions of the air!
Dreadful with banners, fire to slay and parch,
Marching together as the lightnings march,
And swift as storm-clouds. Brazen helms and cars
Clanged to a fierce resurgence of old wars
Above the screaming horns. In state they passed,
Trampling and splendid on and sought the vast—
Rending the darkness like a leaping knife,
The flame, the noble pageant of our life!
The burning seal that stamps man's high indenture
To vain attempt and most forlorn adventure;

Romance, and purple seas, and toppling towns,
And the wind's valiance crying o'er the downs;
That nerves the silly hand, the feeble brain,
From the loose net of words to deeds again
And to all courage! Perilous and sharp
The last chord shook me as wind shakes a harp!
. . . And my friend swung round on his stool, and from gods
    we were men,
"How pretty!" we said; and went on with our talk again.

PORTRAIT OF A BABY

HE LAY within a warm, soft world
Of motion. Colors bloomed and fled,
Maroon and turquoise, saffron, red,
Wave upon wave that broke and whirled
To vanish in the grey-green gloom,
Perspectiveless and shadowy.
A bulging world that had no walls,
A flowing world, most like the sea,
Compassing all infinity
Within a shapeless, ebbing room,
An endless tide that swells and falls . . .
He slept and woke and slept again.
As a veil drops Time dropped away;
Space grew a toy for children's play,
Sleep bolted fast the gates of Sense—
He lay in naked impotence;
Like a drenched moth that creeps and crawls
Heavily up brown, light-baked walls,
To fall in wreck, her task undone,
Yet somehow striving toward the sun.

So, as he slept, his hands clenched tighter,
Shut in the old way of the fighter,
His feet curled up to grip the ground,
His muscles tautened for a bound;
And though he felt, and felt alone,
Strange brightness stirred him to the bone,
Cravings to rise—till deeper sleep
Buried the hope, the call, the leap;
A wind puffed out his mind's faint spark.
He was absorbed into the dark.
He woke again and felt a surge
Within him, a mysterious urge
That grew one hungry flame of passion;
The whole world altered shape and fashion.
Deceived, befooled, bereft and torn,
He scourged the heavens with his scorn,
Lifting a bitter voice to cry
Against the eternal treachery—
Till, suddenly, he found the breast,
And ceased, and all things were at rest,
The earth grew one warm languid sea
And he a wave. Joy, tingling, crept
Throughout him. He was quenched and slept.

So, while the moon made broad her ring,
He slept and cried and was a king.
So, worthily, he acted o'er
The endless miracle once more.
Facing immense adventures daily,
He strove still onward, weeping, gayly,
Conquered or fled from them, but grew
As soil-starved, rough pine-saplings do.
Till, one day, crawling seemed suspect.
He gripped the air and stood erect
And splendid. With immortal rage
He entered on man's heritage!

X—RAY

SMILE if you will or frown, wear silk or serge,
Play age or youth, it will not help, my dear.
This is a place where Truth is made too clear
For idle minds to watch that Truth emerge.
The penetration of this light is just,
Inhuman, and most mercilessly pure.
From its assault upon your house of dust
Only the naked scaffold will endure.

Beneath the perfect candor of this ray
All mortal comeliness lies overthrown,
And even human blood is merely grey,
And ribs and joints are beautiful alone
As the weak flesh contests but cannot stay
The passionless search for the eternal bone.

A MINOR POET

I AM a shell. From me you shall not hear
The splendid trampling of insistent drums,
The orbed gold of the viol's voice that comes,
Heavy with radiance, languorous and clear.
Yet, if you hold me close against the ear,
A dim, far whisper rises clamorously,
The thunderous beat and passion of the sea,
The slow surge of the tides that drown the mere.

Others with subtle hands may pluck the strings,
Making even Love in music audible,
And earth one glory. I am but a shell
That moves, not of itself, and moving sings;
Leaving a fragrance, faint as wine new-shed,
A tremulous murmur from great days long dead.

MORTUARY PARLORS

THE smooth, unobtrusive walls say, "Hush!" in a voice of
    honey and meal,
The refined and comforting chairs protest that sorrow may
    be genteel,
They are all hiding the dead away, they are huddling them
    off to forget . . .
—I would rather scoop a hole in the sand till my hands
    ran blood and sweat,
I would rather raise my friend on a pyre for the lightning to
    do its will,
I would sooner leave my dead to the dogs—they are happy
    over their kill—
Than to bring them here to this oily place to lie like a num-
    bered sheaf!
—This servants' quiet can have no room for my racked
    and horrible grief—
The windows smile with the smiles of masks, the curtains
    are specters walking,
And Death, the obsequious gentleman, comes rubbing
    black gloves and talking!

PORTRAIT OF YOUNG LOVE

If you were with me—as you're not, of course,
I'd taste the elegant tortures of Despair
With a slow, languid, long-refining tongue;
Puzzle for days on one particular stare,
Or if you knew a word's peculiar force,
Or what you looked like when you were quite young.

You'd lift me heaven-high—till a word grated.
Dash me hell-deep—oh that luxurious Pit,
Fatly and well encushioned with self-pity,
Where Love's an epicure not quickly sated!
What mournful musics wander over it,
Faint-blown from some long-lost celestial city!

Such bitter joyousness I'd have, and action,
Were you here—be no more the fool who broods
On true Adventure till he wakes her scorning—
But we're too petty for such noble warning.
And I find just as perfect satisfaction
In analyzing these, and other moods!

[134]

THE GENERAL PUBLIC

"Ah, did you once see Shelley plain?"—BROWNING

"SHELLEY? Oh, yes, I saw him often then,"
The old man said. A dry smile creased his face
With many wrinkles. "That's a great poem, now!
That one of Browning's! Shelley? Shelley plain?
The time that I remember best is this—

"A thin mire crept along the rutted ways,
And all the trees were harried by cold rain
That drove a moment fiercely and then ceased,
Falling so slow it hung like a grey mist
Over the school. The walks were like blurred glass.
The buildings reeked with vapor, black and harsh
Against the deepening darkness of the sky;
And each lamp was a hazy yellow moon,
Filling the space about with golden motes,
And making all things larger than they were.
One yellow halo hung above a door,
That gave on a black passage. Round about
Struggled a howling crowd of boys, pell-mell,

[135]

Pushing and jostling like a stormy sea,
With shouting faces, turned a pasty white
By the strange light, for foam. They all had clods,
Or slimy balls of mud. A few gripped stones.
And there, his back against the battered door,
His pile of books scattered about his feet,
Stood Shelley while two others held him fast,
And the clods beat upon him. 'Shelley! Shelley!'
The high shouts rang through all the corridors,
'Shelley! Mad Shelley! Come along and help!'
And all the crowd dug madly at the earth,
Scratching and clawing at the streaming mud,
And fouled each other and themselves. And still
Shelley stood up. His eyes were like a flame
Set in some white, still room; for all his face
Was white, a whiteness like no human color,
But white and dreadful as consuming fire.
His hands shook now and then, like slender cords
Which bear too heavy weights. He did not speak.
So I saw Shelley plain."
                              "And you?" I said.

"I? I threw straighter than the most of them,
And had firm clods. I hit him—well, at least
Thrice in the face. He made good sport that night."

THE INNOVATOR

(*A Pharaoh Speaks*)

I SAID, "Why should a pyramid
Stand always dully on its base?
I'll change it! Let the top be hid,
The bottom take the apex-place!"
And as I bade they did.

The people flocked in, scores on scores,
To see it balance on its tip.
They praised me with the praise that bores,
My godlike mind on every lip.
—Until it fell, of course.

And then they took my body out
From my crushed palace, mad with rage,
—Well, half the town *was* wrecked, no doubt—
Their crazy anger to assuage
By dragging it about.

[137]

The end? Foul birds defile my skull.
The new king's praises fill the land.
He clings to precept, simple, dull;
His pyramids on bases stand.
But—Lord, how usual!

NOS IMMORTALES

PERHAPS we go with wind and cloud and sun,
Into the free companionship of air;
Perhaps with sunsets when the day is done,
All's one to me—I do not greatly care;
So long as there are brown hills—and a tree
Like a mad prophet in a land of dearth—
And I can lie and hear eternally
The vast monotonous breathing of the earth.

I have known hours, slow and golden-glowing,
Lovely with laughter and suffused with light,
O Lord, in such a time appoint my going,
When the hands clench, and the cold face grows white,
And the spark dies within the feeble brain,
Spilling its star-dust back to dust again.

WORMS' EPIC

BECAUSE all little green things love the sun
They let us travel.
          Slow as moving sand,
Crawling as babies crawl across the floor,
Half-drowning when we burst a drop of dew,
All our new bodies tender with too much light,
We crept out of the rose's burning heart
To a curled petal, paused, and looked about
With fragile, timid eyes at the huge world.

But we were most exploring and untamed
And hardy. When the time had come to fly
We felt a silver shiver in our hearts
Like listening to thunder, and the shock
Cold harpstrings feel under the thrilling hand,
And over us, although we could not see,
Knew the long, delicate, gauzy wings unfold.
Hearts hot as candleflame, eyes wicked with mirth,
We threw ourselves upon the immense, bright air.

What earthquakes and adventures fell on us
In that first second! Mayhem, piracy,
Black murder, featherfoot loving like the touch
Of light on wings, of moon upon the snow!
And through it all the crystal of our flight,
One clear, continual thread.

                A dragonfly
Zoomed over us like a bombing aëroplane,
And we were terrified to death.

                A bird
Snapped up our seven best friends in one quick snatch
And left us shivering.

           A gigantic toad
Gazed at us with great eyes like Arctic moons
And nearly made us goblins.

             And the sun,
That incandescence heavy in the air,
Moved in us like warm sea-water, wave and wave.
And through it all our crystal flight—and love—

The change came. The sky deepened like an eye.
Twilight, the shadowy child, vague as blown smoke,
Called all her furry bats out of their sleep
And ran with them across the darkening fields.

Now we return, tired with the happy day,
And tired with something drowsier than that,
Something too dark and peaceful to be braved,
The immortal sleepiness, the indifferent calm
That makes our minute-selves less than a thought
In a dog's dream, that, like a melting frost,
Runs on the heart in ice.

            And all our sports,
All our mean, gaudy, brave, delightful actions,
Rest like dead children when that quiet touches them.

It does not matter. We will teeter back,
Up the long stalk so long it touches Heaven,
Past the terrific spines, until we lurch,
Dumb with our last exhaustion, walking slow
As crippled gymnasts who've done tricks too long,
Across the living silk of leaf and rose
And then give over utterly. And lie breathless,
While the slow petals close like hands about us
Before Moon waters all heaven with pure light,
In the hushed central chamber, still as sweet thought,
In that secluded crypt, white as new snow.

THE CITY REVISITED

THE grey gulls drift across the bay
Softly and still as flakes of snow
Against the thinning fog. All day
I sat and watched them come and go;
And now at last the sun was set,
Filling the waves with colored fire
Till each seemed like a jeweled spire
Thrust up from some drowned city. Soon
From peak and cliff and minaret
The city's lights began to wink,
Each like a friendly word. The moon
Began to broaden out her shield,
Spurting with silver. Straight before
The brown hills lay like quiet beasts
Stretched out beside a well-loved door,
And filling earth and sky and field
With the calm heaving of their breasts.

Nothing was gone, nothing was changed,
The smallest wave was unestranged
By all the long ache of the years
Since last I saw them, blind with tears.
Their welcome like the hills stood fast:
And I, I had come home at last.

So I laughed out with them aloud
To think that now the sun was broad,
And climbing up the iron sky,
Where the raw streets stretched sullenly
About another room I knew,
In a mean house—and soon there, too,
The smith would burst the flimsy door
And find me lying on the floor.
Just where I fell the other night,
After that breaking wave of pain.
How they will storm and rage and fight,
Servants and mistress, one and all,
"No money for the funeral!"

I broke my life there. Let it stand
At that.
              The waters are a plain,
Heaving and bright on either hand,
A tremulous and lustral peace
Which shall endure though all things cease,
Filling my heart as water fills
A cup. There stand the quiet hills.
So, waiting for my wings to grow,
I watch the gulls sail to and fro,
Rising and falling, soft and swift,
Drifting along as bubbles drift.
And, though I see the face of God

Hereafter—this day have I trod
Nearer to Him than I shall tread
Ever again. The night is dead.
And there's the dawn, poured out like wine
Along the dim horizon-line.
And from the city come the chimes—

We have our heaven on earth—sometimes!

GOING BACK TO SCHOOL

The boat ploughed on. Now Alcatraz was past
And all the grey waves flamed to red again
At the dead sun's last glimmer. Far and vast
The Sausalito lights burned suddenly
In little dots and clumps, as if a pen
Had scrawled vague lines of gold across the hills;
The sky was like a cup some rare wine fills,
And stars came as he watched
                    —and he was free
One splendid instant—back in the great room,
Curled in a chair with all of them beside
And the whole world a rush of happy voices,
With laughter beating in a clamorous tide,
Saw once again the heat of harvest fume
Up to the empty sky in threads like glass,
And ran, and was a part of what rejoices
In thunderous nights of rain; lay in the grass
Sun-baked and tired, looking through a maze
Of tiny stems into a new green world;

[146]

Once more knew eves of perfume, days ablaze
With clear, dry heat on the brown, rolling fields;
Shuddered with fearful ecstasy in bed
Over a book of knights and bloody shields . . .
The ship slowed, jarred and stopped. There, straight ahead,
Were dock and fellows. Stumbling, he was whirled
Out and away to meet them—and his back
Slumped to the old half-cringe, his hands fell slack;
A big boy's arm went round him—and a twist
Sent shattering pain along his tortured wrist,
As a voice cried, a bloated voice and fat,
"Why it's Miss Nancy! Come along, you rat!"

YOUNG BLOOD

*"But, sir," I said, "they tell me the man is like
to die!" The Canon shook his head, indulgently.
"Young blood, Cousin," he boomed. "Young
blood! Youth will be served!"*
—D'HERMONVILLE'S FABLIAUX.

HE WOKE up with a sick taste in his mouth
And lay there heavily, while dancing motes
Whirled through his brain in endless, rippling streams,
And a grey mist weighed down upon his eyes
So that they could not open fully. Yet
After some time his blurred mind stumbled back
To its last ragged memory—a room;
Air foul with wine; a shouting, reeling crowd
Of friends who dragged him, dazed and blind with drink
Out to the street; a crazy rout of cabs;
The steady mutter of his neighbor's voice,
Mumbling out dull obscenity by rote;
And then . . . well, they had brought him home it seemed,
Since he awoke in bed—oh, damn the business!
He had not wanted it—the silly jokes,
"One last, great night of freedom ere you're married!"
"You'll get no fun then!" "H-ssh, don't tell that story,
He'll have a wife soon!"—God! the sitting down
To drink till you were sodden! . . .

                                      Like great light
She came into his thoughts. That was the worst.
To wallow in the mud like this because
His friends were fools. He was not fit to touch,
To see, oh far, far off, that silver place
Where God stood manifest to man in her. . . .
Fouling himself. . . . One thing he brought to her,
At least. He had been clean; had taken it
A kind of point of honor from the first.
Others might wallow but he didn't care
For those things. . . .
                        Suddenly his vision cleared.
And something seemed to grow within his mind.
Something was wrong—the color of the wall—
The queer shape of the bedposts—everything
Was changed, somehow . . . his room. Was this his room?

. . . He turned his head—and saw beside him there
The sagging body's slope, the paint-smeared face,
And the loose, open mouth, lax and awry,
The breasts, the bleached and brittle hair . . . these things.
. . . As if all Hell were crushed to one bright line
Of lightning for a moment. Then he sank,
Prone beneath an intolerable weight.
And bitter loathing crept up all his limbs.

THE BREAKING POINT

IT WAS not when temptation came,
Swiftly and blastingly as flame,
And seared me white with burning scars;
When I stood up for age-long wars
And held the very Fiend at grips;
When all my mutinous body rose
To range itself beside my foes,
And, like a greyhound in the slips,
The Beast that dwells within me roared,
Lunging and straining at his cord. . . .
For all the blusterings of Hell,
It was not then I slipped and fell;
For all the storm, for all the hate,
I kept my soul inviolate.

But when the fight was fought and won,
And there was Peace as still as Death
On everything beneath the sun.
Just as I started to draw breath,

And yawn, and stretch, and pat myself,
—The grass began to whisper things—
And every tree became an elf,
That grinned and chuckled counselings:
Birds, beasts, one thing alone they said,
Beating and dinning at my head.
I could not fly. I could not shun it.
Slimily twisting, slow and blind,
It crept and crept into my mind.
Whispered and shouted, sneered and laughed,
Screamed out until my brain was daft,
One snaky word, *"What if you'd done it?"*
And I began to think . . .

                            Ah, well,
What matter how I slipped and fell?
Or you, you gutter-searcher, say!
Tell where you found me yesterday!

LONELY BURIAL

THERE were not many at that lonely place,
Where two scourged hills met in a little plain.
The wind cried loud in gusts, then low again.
Three pines strained darkly, runners in a race
Unseen by any. Toward the further woods
A dim harsh noise of voices rose and ceased.
—We were most silent in those solitudes—
Then, sudden as a flame, the black-robed priest,

The clotted earth piled roughly up about
The hacked red oblong of the new-made thing,
Short words in swordlike Latin—and a rout
Of dreams most impotent, unwearying.
Then, like a blind door shut on a carouse,
The terrible bareness of the soul's last house.

POOR DEVIL!

WELL, I was tired of life; the silly folk,
The tiresome noises, all the common things
I loved once, crushed me with an iron yoke.
I longed for the cool quiet and the dark,
Under the common sod where louts and kings
Lie down, serene, unheeding, careless, stark,
Never to rise or move or feel again,
Filled with the ecstasy of being dead. . . .

I put the shining pistol to my head
And pulled the trigger hard—I felt no pain,
No pain at all; the pistol had missed fire
I thought; then, looking at the floor, I saw
My huddled body lying there—and awe
Swept over me. I trembled—and looked up.
About me was—not that, my heart's desire,
That small and dark abode of death and peace—
But all from which I sought a vain release!
The sky, the people and the staring sun
Glared at me as before. I was undone.

[153]

My last state ten times worse than was my first.
Helpless, I stood, befooled, betrayed, accursed,
Fettered to Life forever, horribly;
Caught in the meshes of Eternity,
No further doors to break or bars to burst.

GHOSTS
OF A LUNATIC ASYLUM

HERE, where men's eyes were empty and as bright
As the blank windows set in glaring brick,
When the wind strengthens from the sea—and night
Drops like a fog and makes the breath come thick;

By the deserted paths, the vacant halls,
One may see figures, twisted shades and lean,
Like the mad shapes that crawl an Indian screen,
Or paunchy smears you find on prison walls.

Turn the knob gently! There's the Thumbless Man,
Still weaving glass and silk into a dream,
Although the wall shows through him—and the Khan
Journeys Cathay beside a paper stream.

A Rabbit Woman chitters by the door—
—Chilly the grave-smell comes from the turned sod—
Come—lift the curtain—and be cold before
The silence of the eight men who were God!

[155]

THE QUALITY OF COURAGE

Black trees against an orange sky,
Trees that the wind shook terribly,
Like a harsh spume along the road,
Quavering up like withered arms,
Writhing like streams, like twisted charms
Of hot lead flung in snow. Below
The iron ice stung like a goad,
Slashing the torn shoes from my feet,
And all the air was bitter sleet.

And all the land was cramped with snow,
Steel-strong and fierce and glimmering wan,
Like pale plains of obsidian.
—And yet I strove—and I was fire
And ice—and fire and ice were one
In one vast hunger of desire.
A dim desire, of pleasant places,
And lush fields in the summer sun,
And logs aflame, and walls, and faces,
—And wine, and old ambrosial talk,

And unforgotten hands—and looks,
Drawn together, eyes and eyes
By the old, blind sorceries
Into the intense, the cloudless blue,
Till two souls were one, and flame,
And the flesh that has no name.
But for the most I thought of heat,
Desiring greatly. . . . Hot white sand
The lazy body lies at rest in,
Or sun-dried, scented grass to nest in,
And fires, innumerable fires,
Great fagots hurling golden gyres
Of sparks far up, and the red heart
In sea-coals, crashing as they part
To tiny flares, and kindling snapping,
Bunched sticks that burst their string and wrapping
And fall like jackstraws; green and blue
The evil flames of driftwood too,
And heavy, sullen lumps of coke
With still, fierce heat and ugly smoke. . . .
. . . And then the shape of my disgrace
And my sin came like a sword,
Thrice, to the heart—and as I fell
I thought I saw a light before.

I woke. My hands were blue and sore,
Torn on the ice. I scarcely felt
The frozen sleet begin to melt
Upon my face as I breathed deeper,
But lay there warmly, like a sleeper
Who shifts his arm once, and moans low,
And then sinks back to night. Slow, slow,
And still as Death, came Sleep and Death
And looked at me with quiet breath.
Unbending figures, black and stark
Against the intense deeps of the dark,

Tall as old pines. Like sweet and fire
Rest crept and crept along my veins,
Gently. And there were no more pains. . . .

Was it not better so to lie?
The fight was done. Even gods tire
Of fighting. . . . My way was the wrong.
Now I should drift and drift along
To endless quiet, golden peace,
And let the tortured body cease.

And then a light winked like an eye.
. . . And very many miles away
A girl stood at a warm, lit door,
Holding a lamp. Ray upon ray
It cloaked the snow with perfect light.
And where she was there was no night
Nor could be, ever. God is sure,
And in his hands are things secure.
It is not given me to trace
The lovely laughter of that face,
Like a clear brook most full of light,
Or olives swaying on a height,
So silver they have wings, almost;
Like a great word once known and lost
And meaning all things. Nor her voice
A happy sound where larks rejoice,
Her body, that great loveliness,
The tender fashion of her dress,
I may not paint them.
                              These I see,
Blazing through all eternity,
A fire-winged sign, a glorious tree!

She stood there, and at once I knew
The bitter thing that I must do.

There could be no surrender now;
Though Sleep and Death were whispering low.
My way was wrong. So. Would it mend
If I shrank back before the end
And sank to death and cowardice?
No, the last lees must be drained up,
Base wine from an ignoble cup;
(Yet not so base as sleek content
When I had shrunk from punishment)
The wretched body strain anew!
Life was a storm to wander through.
I took the wrong way. Good and well,
At least my feet sought out not Hell.
Though night were one consuming flame
I must go on for my base aim,
And so, perhaps, make evil grow
To something clean by agony
And reach that light upon the snow . . .
And touch her dress at last . . .

                    So, so,
I crawled. I could not speak or see
Save dimly. The ice glared like fire,
A long bright Hell of choking cold,
And each vein was a tautened wire,
Throbbing with torture—and I crawled.
My hands were wounds.

                  So I attained
The second Hell. The snow was stained
I thought, and shook my head at it
How red it was! Black tree-roots clutched
And tore—and soon the snow was smutched
Anew; and I lurched babbling on,
And then fell down to rest a bit,
And came upon another Hell,
Loose stones with ice made terrible,
To roll and gash men as they fell.

I stumbled, slipped . . . and all was gone
That I had gained. Once more I lay
Before the long bright Hell of ice.
And still the light was far away.
There was red mist before my eyes
Or I could tell you how I went
Across the swaying firmament,
A glittering torture of cold stars,
And how I fought in Titan wars . . .
And died . . . and lived again upon
The rack . . . and how the horses strain
When their red task is nearly done. . . .

I only know that there was Pain,
Infinite and eternal Pain.
And that I fell—and rose again.

So she was walking in the road.
And I stood upright like a man,
Once, and fell blind, and heard her cry . . .
And then there came long agony.

There was no pain when I awoke,
No pain at all. Rest, like a goad,
Spurred my eyes open—and light broke
Upon them like a million swords:
And she was there. There are no words.

Heaven is for a moment's span.
And ever.
        So I spoke and said,
"My honor stands up unbetrayed,
And I have seen you. Dear . . ."
                     Sharp pain
Closed like a cloak. . . .
             I moaned and died.

Here, even here, these things remain.
I shall draw nearer to her side.

Oh dear and laughing, lost to me,
Hidden in grey Eternity,
The ages crumble down like dust,
Dark roses, deviously thrust
And scattered in sweet wine—but I,
I shall lift up to you my cry,
And kiss your cool lips presently
Beneath the ever-living Tree.

This in my heart I keep for goad!
Somewhere, in Heaven she walks that road.
Somewhere . . . in Heaven . . . she walks . . . that . . .
    road. . . .

THE LOVER IN HELL

ETERNALLY the choking steam goes up
From the black pools of seething oil. . . .

How merry
Those little devils are! They've stolen the pitchfork
From Bel, there, as he slept. Look!—oh look, look!
They've got at Nero! Oh it isn't fair!
Lord, how he squeals! Stop it . . . it's, well—indecent!
But funny! . . . See, Bel's waked. They'll catch it now!

. . . Eternally that stifling reek arises,
Blotting the dome with smoky, terrible towers,
Black, strangling trees, whispering obscene things
Amongst their branches, clutching with maimed hands,
Or oozing slowly, like blind tentacles
Up to the gates; higher than that heaped brick
Man piled to smite the sun. And all around
Are devils. One can laugh . . . but that hunched shape
The face one stone, like those Assyrian kings
One sees in carvings, watching men flayed red

Horribly laughable in leaps and writhes;
That face—utterly evil, clouded round
With evil like a smoke—it turns smiles sour!
. . . And Nero there, the flabby cheeks astrain
And sweating agony . . . long agony . . .
Imperishable, unappeasable
Forever . . . well . . . it droops the mouth. Till I
Look up.
          There's one blue patch no smoke dares touch.
Sky, clear, ineffable, alive with light,
Always the same.
                Before, I never knew
Rest and green peace.
                She stands there in the sun.
It seems so quaint she should have long gold wings.
I never have got used—folded across
Her breast, or fluttering with fierce, pure light,
Like shaken steel. Her crown, too. Well, it's queer!
And then she never cared much for the harp
On earth. Here, though . . .
                She is all peace, all quiet,
All passionate desires, the eloquent thunder
Of new, glad suns, shouting aloud for joy,
Over fresh worlds and clean, trampling the air
Like stooping hawks, to the long wind of horns,
Flung from the bastions of Eternity.
And she is the low lake, drowsy and gentle,
And good words spoken from the tongues of friends,
And calmness in the evening, and deep thoughts,
Falling like dreams from the stars' solemn mouths.
All these.
          They said she was unfaithful once.
Or I remembered it—and so, for that,
I lie here, I suppose. Yes, so they said.
You see she is so troubled, looking down,
Sorrowing deeply for my torments. I

Of course, feel nothing while I see her—save
That sometimes when I think the matter out,
And what earth-people said of us, of her,
It seems as if I must be, here, in Heaven,
And she—
               Then I grow proud; and suddenly
There comes a splatter of oil against my skin,
Hurting this time. And I forget my pride:
And my face writhes.
                    Some day the little ladder
Of white words that I build up, up, to her
May fetch me out. Meanwhile it isn't bad. . . .

But what a sense of humor God must have!

ELEGY FOR AN ENEMY

(*For G. H.*)

SAY, does that stupid earth
Where they have laid her,
Bind still her sullen mirth,
Mirth which betrayed her?
Do the lush grasses hold,
Greenly and glad,
That brittle-perfect gold
She alone had?

Smugly the common crew,
Over their knitting,
Mourn her—as butchers do
Sheep-throats they're slitting.
She was my enemy,
One of the best of them.
Would she come back to me,
God damn the rest of them!

Damn them, the flabby, fat,
Sleek little darlings!
We gave them tit for tat,
Snarlings for snarlings.
Squashy pomposities,
Shocked at our violence,
Let not one tactful hiss
Break her new silence!

Maids of antiquity,
Look well upon her;
Ice was her chastity,
Spotless her honor.
Neighbors, with breasts of snow,
Dames of much virtue,
How she could flame and glow!
Lord, how she hurt you!

She was a woman, and
Tender—at times.
(Delicate was her hand)
One of her crimes!
Hair that strayed elfinly,
Lips red as haws,
You, with the ready lie,
Was that the cause?

Rest you, my enemy,
Slain without fault.
Life smacks but tastelessly
Lacking your salt.
Stuck in a bog whence naught
May catapult me,
Come from the grave, long-sought,
Come and insult me!

We knew that sugared stuff
Poisoned the other;
Rough as the wind is rough,
Sister and brother.
Breathing the ether clear
Others forlorn have found—
Oh, for that peace austere
She and her scorn have found!

VII LYRICS AND SONGS

FLOOD-TIDE

(*Maine Coast*)

1917

I DID *not make the song for honor or hardihood,*
Nor from boy's love did I make it, when that blew hot and cold;
But the tide had risen about us, the deep, encompassing flood
And we were alive to see it, before our flesh grew old.

There was moon like a spilling of milky sap from the sky
And the tree of the sky was a candle of creamy flame,
Each white-fire-leaf of a star distinct; and old wind went by
Hooded in dark and ashamed as it whispered some mutter-
  ing name.

We were huddled up in the launch like a sleepy parcel of
  birds.
The plunging silence engulfed us. We heard, as if we had
  died,
The throb of the engine's heart erase our tiptoeing words,
And the slow mysterious mouth of the water against the
  side.

[171]

If you dripped your fingers awave, wet star-dust clung to
the skin,
Spangling the wax-cool hand with the pollen and seeds of
dawn,
And the wake, like a fish of fire, went twisting alive within
The willow-dark cage of green, and in splinters of foam
was gone.

Then we saw the cloudy old house, and the waters deep
at its stair,
Bright in an endless flood, irradiate, calm and wise,
Like the milk-white body of Truth asleep in her naked hair,
And the blood and strength of the Earth arose to our
dazzling eyes!

Quiet, quiet and quiet, said the march of the wave beneath.
Oh, immaculate shone the mind while the lotos of silence
grew!
And the sore heart heavy with youth was a clean blade
straight in its sheath,
As we drank with a matchless dream in that chrism of salt
and dew.

After the thirteenth year, the water runs as before,
The gemmed wave in the water, the starlight on the gem,
All but the crew who sailed there, and they return no more,
But the words are as they were written. I cannot alter
them.

1930

EXPRESSIONS
NEAR THE END OF WINTER

IF I but had my longing! not opals sad and rare,
For noble stones are proud things, and best befit your hair;
Not purple-buttoned waistcoats, nor sack to drink me
   deep,
But white, smooth sheets to lie in—oh I'd sleep, sleep,
   sleep!

And the corners of that bedstead should be olivewood so
   green,
And the gentle swan's-down pillows should have com-
   forted a queen;
With a canopy above me, of azure silk outspréad,
Four carved evangels at my feet and magi at my head!

And no sun should creep there, and but small starlight,
And the whole room be odorous of gardens known at night;
The thick scents of evening, the attar of the rose,
Should take away my weariness both drowsily and close.

You would come on tiptoe, like the whisper of birds' wings,
With a quite small music and some occupying things,
And draw up close a cushion, and bend a cautious ear,
And say, "Now don't disturb him—for he's tired, poor
dear!"

And then, both handfast, we would dream long days,
Till the dry world shimmered to a sleepy, happy haze.
With no cares to speak of—no silly fools to fret—
Oh my great, proud longing that I'll never, never get!

SNOWFALL

HEAVEN is hell, if it be as they say,
An endless day.
A pen of terrible radiance, on whose walls
No shadow falls,
No sunset ever comes because no sun has ever risen,
Where, like bewildered flies,
Poor immortalities
Interminably crawl, caught in a crystal prison.

Yet, if there is but night to recompense
Impertinence,
How can we bear to live so long and know
The end is so?
Creatures that hate the dark, to utmost dark descending?
The worm's dull enmity,
To feel it—but not see!
To be afraid at night and know that night unending!

[175]

There is a time when, though the sun be weak,
It is not bleak
With perfect and intolerable light,
Nor has the night
Yet put those eyes to sleep that do not wish for slumber;
When, on the city we know,
The pale, transmuting snow
Falls softly, in sighing flakes, immaculate, without num-
ber.

Whisperingly it drifts, and whisperingly
Fills earth and sky
With fragile petals, tranquil as a swan's
Blanch pinions.
And where it falls is silence, subtle and mild.
That silence is not cruel
But calm as a frozen jewel,
And clasped to its cold frail breast Earth sucks in rest like
a child.

If there can be a heaven, let it wear
Even such an air.
Not shamed with sun nor black without a ray,
But gently day.
A tired street, whereon the snow falls, whitely,
An infant, cradled in fleece,
An ancient, drowsy with peace,
Unutterable peace, too pure to shine too brightly.

SONG

Be at peace, and let the gale
Shake blossom down from the chestnut tree
And the light rain tear the blossom apart.
There is no hatred in the May rain.
It will fall to-day and another day,
Washing the bud and the barren spike
And the worm's body, all alike,
With neither malice nor tenderness.
There was a time when every drop
Fell like a weapon upon the heart
Until it seemed that the heart must stop.
But the body has known its enemy,
The heart has eaten its bitterness;
There is nothing more for the heart to say.

Be at peace, we have stolen away,
We have stolen our life again,
We shall sleep to-night in spite of the gale.
Rest as quiet and sleep as sound
As the dead sleep in the living ground.

Do not fear for the steadfast heart,
Do not fear for the chestnut bloom
Although the waters tear it apart,
We have shut Death's lips with a country tale.

HANDS

My wife's hands are long and thin,
Fit to catch a spirit in,
Fit to set a subtle snare
For something lighter than the air.

My brother's hands are long and fine,
Good at verse and pouring wine,
Good to spend and bad to hoard
And good to hold a singing sword.

My own hands are short and blunt
Being children of affront,
Base mechanics at the most
That have sometimes touched a ghost.

I ask between the running sands,
A blessing upon four hands,
And for mine an iron stake
They can do their best to break.

Now God the Son and God the Sire
And God the triple-handed fire,
Make these blessings come to be
Out of your civility
For four hands of courtesy.

Amen.

LOVE IN TWILIGHT

THERE is darkness behind the light—and the pale light
    drips
Cold on vague shapes and figures that, half-seen, loom
Like the carven prows of proud, far-triumphing ships—
And the firelight wavers and changes about the room,

As the three logs crackle and burn with a small still sound;
Half-blotting with dark the deeper dark of her hair,
Where she lies, head pillowed on arm, and one hand curved
    round
To shield the white face and neck from the faint thin
    glare.

Gently she breathes—and the long limbs lie at ease,
And the rise and fall of the young, slim, virginal breast
Is as certain-sweet as the march of slow wind through
    trees,
Or the great soft passage of clouds in a sky at rest.

I kneel, and our arms enlace, and we kiss long, long.
I am drowned in her as in sleep. There is no more pain.
Only the rustle of flames like a broken song
That rings half-heard through the dusty halls of the
    brain.

One shaking and fragile moment of ecstasy,
While the grey gloom flutters and beats like an owl above.
And I would not move or speak for the sea or the sky
Or the flame-bright wings of the miraculous Dove!

THE SONG OF COLD AND PAIN

COLDER than leopards' eyes the arc
Where all the freezing stars go round,
Black wind runs trotting to the dark,
Striking cold hoofs on the cold ground.

The body crawls, the sinews scrape,
Knotted and cramped by fingering cold;
It shrinks my flesh into the shape
I shall not break from when I'm old.

And yet my shoulders lift the air
That weighs like ice, that pours like lead,
For cold's a thing the flesh can bear
If desperation's in the head.

The wooden head needs other pyres.
To warm alive its wooden wits,
But in this cold there are more fires
Than ever burnt a sun to bits!

Inside of cold, inside of pain,
Past each last tingle of the sense,
The flame called God ascends again
In all its raging innocence.

It is the scarlets of the white,
It is the seeing of the blind,
More furiously clear than light
It burns like snow upon the mind.

I built my house with Pain for wall,
I filled its halls with Cold for wives,
And twenty years have bade it fall
And it shall stand for twenty lives.

I hung the doors with griefs I had,
Fear was a grape I crushed to wine,
And not an angel good or bad,
Can boast such feasting as is mine!

The fire that on my hearth exults
But Pain and Cold could throw and tame
Till now I know in every pulse
The last intensity of flame.

In that excruciating joy
Have Cold and Pain my judgment writ,
Though it exalt me or destroy
I must arise and follow it!

Life is a vapor, dreaming South,
A sleepy field 'twixt stream and stream.
Death is a dream that shuts the mouth
—Until you live inside the dream.

ROAD AND HILLS

I SHALL go away
To the brown hills, the quiet ones,
The vast, the mountainous, the rolling,
Sun-fired and drowsy!

My horse snuffs delicately
At the strange wind;
He settles to a swinging trot; his hoofs tramp the dust.
The road winds, straightens,
Slashes a marsh,
Shoulders out a bridge,
Then—
Again the hills.
Unchanged, innumerable,
Bowing huge, round backs;
Holding secret, immense converse
In gusty voices;
Fruitful, fecund, toiling
Like yoked black oxen.

The clouds pass like great, slow thoughts
And vanish
In the intense blue.

My horse lopes; the saddle creaks and sways.
A thousand glittering spears of sun slant from on high.
The immensity, the spaces,
Are like the spaces
Between star and star.

The hills sleep.
If I put my hand on one,
I would feel the vast heave of its breath.
I would start away before it awakened
And shook the world from its shoulders.
A cicada's cry deepens the hot silence.

The hills open
To show a slope of poppies,
Ardent, noble, heroic,
A flare, a great flame of orange;
Giving sleepy, brittle scent
That stings the lungs.
A creeping wind slips through them like a ferret; they
    bow and dance, answering Beauty's voice . . .

The horse whinnies. I dismount
And tie him to the grey worn fence.
I set myself against the javelins of grass and sun
And climb the rounded breast,
That flows like a sea-wave.
The summit crackles with heat, there is no shelter, no
    hollow from the flagellating glare.

I lie down and look at the sky, shading my eyes.
My body becomes strange, the sun takes it and changes it,
    it does not feel, it is like the body of another.
The air blazes. The air is diamond.
Small noises move among the grass . . .

Blackly,
A hawk mounts, mounts in the inane
Seeking the star-road,
Seeking the end . . .
But there is no end.

Here, in this light, there is no end. . . .

ANCIENT'S SONG

SPRING, Summer, Fall,
I have watched and counted them all
Like sheep into a fold.
And now, if at the last,
The sky is overcast
And the stream runs thin and cold.
I cannot hate this winter on the stream,
If 'twas a dream, it was a lordly dream
And men are right to die when they are old.

BAD DREAM

OUT of the stroke, the change,
The body locked in its death
Like a stream locked in the ice,
The whiteness under the cheek,
The lips forever set
In the look that is always strange
Because we remember yet
How they spoke, how the mere breath
Was enough to make them speak.

I saw the soul arise,
Naked, shaped like a blade,
Free, inhuman and bright,
And where the body was laid
I saw it hover.
It had no need of eyes.
It had forgotten the grief,
The long pain and the brief,
The daybreak, the burning night,
The touch of water and light.
These were over.

It was free. It would not return.
I saw its brightness spurn
Like the heel of a fugitive
The body it hung above,
The body which gave it birth—
It is this I cannot forgive.
It is thus they answer our love
When they are gone from the earth.

CHIPS
FROM AN ANTIQUE QUARRY

ANNA MIRANDA

PERPLEXED by futures seen too clear,
After a little life of mirth,
Anna Miranda offers here
Her celibate body to the earth.

She was too fond to live alone
But lovers only made her sad.
—She never loosed the virgin zone.
And wished her mother never had.

MID-OCEAN

Oh travelers who feel uneasy,
Pause, and admire the irony.
John, whom the rocking of a chair made queasy,
Buried at sea!

I read my eyes away in seeking God,
But He was difficult, and hard to find.
Now He is here, about me, in the sod.
And I am blind.

TWO LOVERS

What were you once? *A woman*. And you came—?
Loving you, hither. Strange! for now we lie
At peace, I do not even know your name.
Nor I.

GREEK CHILD

Clay returning to the clay,
Zoe lies and never stirs,
Although we sacrificed each day
A little doe with eyes like hers.

A LOVER

All my long youth I worshipped lovely Corinna
As a divine thing.
Having enjoyed her at last, and found her a woman,
I sleep in darkness.

A YOUTH

So cleanly formed, in mind and limb,
Paul seemed an answer sent to prayers.
His parents centered all on him
And did not seek for later heirs.

Now, in the morning of his day,
He rests beneath this cypress-bough,
Leaving his parents sad—and they
Cannot have other children now.

EGO

Well begun is nearly done.
(*Blow the taper—bolt the door!*)
But Tom, Tom, the piper's son,
Can't begin it any more.

VIII THE KINGDOM OF THE MAD

FOR ALL BLASPHEMERS

Adam was my grandfather,
A tall, spoiled child,
A red, clay tower
In Eden, green and mild.
He ripped the Sinful Pippin
From its sanctimonious limb.
Adam was my grandfather—
And I take after him.

Noah was my uncle
And he got dead drunk.
There were planets in his liquor-can
And lizards in his bunk.
He fell into the Bottomless
Past Hell's most shrinking star.
Old Aunt Fate has often said
How much alike we are.

[197]

Lilith, she's my sweetheart
Till my heartstrings break,
Most of her is honey-pale
And all of her is snake.
Sweet as secret thievery,
I kiss her all I can,
While Somebody Above remarks
"That's not a nice young man!"

Bacchus was my brother,
Nimrod is my friend.
All of them have talked to me
On how such courses end.
But when His Worship takes me up
How can I fare but well?
For who in gaudy Hell will care?
—And I shall be in Hell.

LOST

WITH a start I arose where the moon waved pale on my
    bed—
For the night rang out to a clamor like desolate gulls,
To the pallid dispute of the chittering souls of the dead
Wizenedly seething afar in a river of skulls.

And "We are betrayed!" said one, and "Eternity
Is lost! Eternity's lost!" in the voice of dim rain,
And the twilight of answering shadows took up the cry
"Eternity's lost!" and they rustled like leaves again.

I shuddered and crept to the warmth and the idle dream,
But through all the long stupor of night they quavered
    at me,
Wailing like withered-up reeds in the drought of a stream,
Crying like birds for forgotten Eternity.

DINNER
IN A QUICK LUNCH ROOM

Soup should be heralded with a mellow horn,
Blowing clear notes of gold against the stars;
Strange *entrées* with a jangle of glass bars
Fantastically alive with subtle scorn;
Fish, by a plopping, gurgling rush of waters,
Clear, vibrant waters, beautifully austere;
Roast, with a thunder of drums to stun the ear,
A screaming fife, a voice from ancient slaughters!

Over the salad let the woodwinds moan;
Then the green silence of many watercresses;
Dessert, a balalaika, strummed alone;
Coffee, a slow, low singing no passion stresses;
Such are my thoughts as—clang! crash! bang!—I brood
And gorge the sticky mess these fools call food!

LUNCH AT A CITY CLUB

(For, though not to, D. M. C.)

THE member with the face like a pale ham
Settles his stomachs in the leather chair.
The member with the mustard-colored hair
Chats with the member like a curly ram,
Then silence like the shutting of a clam,
Gulps, and slow eating, and the waiters' stare—
Like prosperous leeches settling to their fare
The members gorge, distending as they cram.

And I am fiery ice—and a hand knocks
Inside my heart. Three hours till God comes true,
When there's no earth or sky or time in clocks
But only hell and paradise and you.
Life bows his strings! I shout the amazing tune!
. . . The dullest member drops his coffee spoon.

DEVOURER OF NATIONS

"Strength shall be thrust to the Eater,
And down to the Strong One, sweet."
Was ever a proverb neater,
A phrasing more apt, or meeter,
To fix on our Course-Completer
As we end Life's beat?

You'll decorate quite the scarlet
And secret hall of his tongue—
With your clasped hands marble and chilly,
And your face like a frozen lily—
For Death is a luscious varlet,
And likes maids young.

So there's the end of it, Nelly,
Of you and your purple hat!
And I, your impotent Shelley,
With czars and pariahs smelly,
Shall tapestry well his belly,
That gray, round Rat!

[202]

ARCHITECTS

My son has built a fortified house
To keep his pride from the thunder,
And his steadfast heart from the gnawing mouse
That nibbles the roots of wonder.

My daughter's wit has hammered and filed
Her slight and glittering armor.
She hides in its rings like a dragon-child,
And nothing on earth can harm her.

My wife has molded a coffin of lead
From the counterfeit tears of mourners.
She rests in it, calm as a saint long dead,
And the Four Winds kneel at its corners.

I have scooped my den with a crafty thumb
In the guts of an arid acre.
And it may not last till Kingdom Come
—But it will not cripple its maker.

It is six feet long by three feet deep
And some may call it narrow.
But, when I get into it, I can keep
The nakedness of an arrow.

ABRAHAM'S BOSOM

So THE world darkened, as if ink were poured
Over a picture, clotting jammily;
And there was really nothing left to see,
And I was just beginning to feel bored
—They might have let me drive the hearse at least!
I'd love to dangle on the plumes and kick
Fat-vested mourners—when, in half a tick,
Light gurgled from the sky and filled the East.

I walked on something squashy like a tire,
Rebounding heavily where'er I trod,
Set with black plants that grew like tangled wire . . .
I'd just begun to look around for God,
When mountains fell, the skies gaped crimson-shot
And thunder took the earth. . . .
                        A voice said, *"Vot?"*

PROHIBITION

"I WOULDN'T mind if it were gin!" he said,
"Good gin's like ether, sick, with pungent sweet,
And rum I never liked—not even neat.
Champagne and such stuck pins into my head.
Old port was sunlight where a ruby bled.
The silky-bright liqueurs had twinkling feet
Like gipsy children running down a street;
And beer's as old a brother as good bread.

"Still, I could give them up!" he mused and sighed
Like a poor scrawny gust of city wind,
"But it's the precedent that's bad! You'll find
Things worse Hereafter . . . I'd a friend who died.
And . . . well, damned souls had never much to tell . . .
But now they've stopped the Lethe, down in Hell."

NEARSIGHT

WHEN Spruggles takes his glasses off, he sees.
Globular people strut like walking trees
Through a strange, oozy mist that melts to air
Some thirty feet before his blinking stare
And all the edgy corners of the streets
Are puffed and bulged like bottle-'scaped Afreets!
—There are no definitions. All is dim.
A yellow underworld, where trolleys swim
Enormous as a magic, and the least
Rice-powdered shop-girl, like a vesting priest
Assumes estranged beauty, cloudy-far,
Desirous as a water-mirrored star.
—The houses are cartoons—So is his wife—
He thinks "Grotesque" would be the word for Life.

BEFORE MICHAEL'S LAST FIGHT

The lightning quivers up in Gabriel's hand,
Whetting his sword on a bleak ridge of cloud,
And all the stars of hell are crying loud
At the bright insult of that sparking brand.
The demon-torn and devastated land
Smokes like a field of salt wild fire has plowed,
Athwart it towers Satan, thunder-browed,
Black at his side his Princely Evils stand.

After our fated triumph, some will drink,
Those who had girls will kiss the girls they had;
But I shall wander on the starry brink
And feel divine, and, beautifully sad,
Sing my one song about you to the void;
And make the angels horribly annoyed.

UNFAMILIAR QUARTET

THE concert-hall creaked like a full-dress shirt
As the happy audience hugged its musical smart,
And waited to be titillatingly hurt
By the pelting of the over-ripe fruit of Art.

The violin wept its sugar, the saxophone
Howled like a mandrake raped by a lightning-stroke,
The 'cello gave a blond and stomachy groan—
And then the hard bugle spoke.

Sewing a wound together with brazen stitches,
Stitching a bronze device on the rotten skin,
And calling the elegant audience sons of bitches,
It ceased, and the sons of bitches
Applauded the violin.

OPERATION

(For J. F. C., Jr.)

BOUND to the polished table, arm and leg,
I lay and watched, with loud, disgusting fear,
The army of the instruments draw near,
Hook, saw, sleek scissor and distorted peg;
My eyes were like a spaniel's when they beg,
The nurses' purpose was so very clear
. . . And though I tried to bite one in the ear
She stayed as white and silent as an egg.

Time, the superb physician, drew his breath,
"I'll just remove Youth, Health and Love," he said,
"The rest is for Consulting-Surgeon Death."
God, how I hated that peremptory head!
As through the ether came his sickening drawl
"Now this won't hurt. . . . Oh, it won't hurt at all."

THE TRAPEZE PERFORMER

(*For C. M.*)

FIERCE little bombs of gleam snap from his spangles,
Sleek flames glow softly on his silken tights,
The waiting crowd blurs to crude darks and whites
Beneath the lamps that stare like savage bangles;
Safe in a smooth and sweeping arc he dangles
And sees the tanbark tower like old heights
Before careening eyes. At last he sights
The waiting hands and sinuously untangles.

Over the sheer abyss so deadly-near,
He falls, like wine to its appointed cup,
Turns like a wheel of fireworks, and is mine.
Battering hands acclaim our triumph clear.
—And steadfast muscles draw my sonnet up
To the firm iron of the fourteenth line.

JUDGMENT

"HE'LL let us off with fifty years!" one said.
And one, "I always knew that Bible lied!"
One who was philanthropic stood aside,
Patting his sniveling virtues on the head.
"Yes, there may be some—pain," another wheezed.
"One rending touch to fit the soul for bliss."
"A bare formality!" one seemed to hiss.
And everyone was pink and fed and pleased.

Then thunder came, and with an earthquake sound
Shook those fat corpses from their flabby languor.
The sky was furious with immortal anger,
We miserable sinners hugged the ground:
Seeing through all the torment, saying, "Yes,"
God's quiet face, serenely merciless.

BOARDING-HOUSE HALL

FIRST the stuffy upholstered smell of the chairs began
To puff a few sighs of dust, and the sticky-varnished
Reek of the cheap worn wood had a verse to scan
About Love and Death and Beauty, fly-spotted and tar-
    nished.

"I never liked her at all!" said a green glass bowl,
And a whiff of anger whitened the broken plaster,
"Her eyes were too big!" cried a smell with paws like a
    mole.
"She was slinky," the pinks spoke. "Thin," creaked a
    broken castor.

"She was greedy. She never loved him. She powdered her
    nose."
Pale-calm as a specter's gem in the shadow-playtime,
The ghost of the perfume hid in her hair arose
And shook dark wealth from its robes and possessed the
    day-time.

Like a scented tree of Egypt it burgeoned above,
For a space of quiet like myrrh, for the flash of a
feather.
They were still, who had seen the dead, happy face of
Love...
—And the smells of the onions trooped up the stairs to-
gether.

BLOOD BROTHERS

THE blunt snouts of a dozen worms or so
Were busy at the thing that had worn clothes,
As conscientious as a lot of clowns
And quite as self-absorbed.
                              Beside the grave
A figure stood in armor, stood and blazed
With the pale dazzle of an April moon,
Rippling a steely silver from his wings
That trembled in their fierce desire for air;
Armed like an angel, blazoned like a king,
And proud as charging seas first seen at dawn.
The worms raised up their heads and spoke to him.
He answered like a father to his children,
Praising them all for honest, quiet work,
And pointing out new pastures.
                              And they bowed;
Again became a stir among corruption.
He looked upon the seethe with steady eyes
Of awful friendship.
                    So I left them there,
The three immortal parts of John J. Jones.

WATCHMEN

Six of us were your guards, slayers of fear,
Humor, the parti-colored, juggling knives,
Rhyme with a sonnet train of elfin wives,
Friendship, as solid-indolent as beer;
Love with his harp you thought a trifle queer,
But most amusing—if he walked in gyves.
Trust and myself made pillows of our lives.
And so you bore with us for quite a year.

You wearied. Humor twinkled to a star.
Rhyme turned a broker and began to add.
I'm sure that Friendship went entirely mad;
And Love crept stalely drunk from bar to bar.
Only remained the bald old dog, blind Trust
And I—and we shall growl till both are dust.

POSITIVELY
THE LAST PERFORMANCE

So HERE's an end—and all the truth of you
Is said that can be said—and all the lies.
Clear for the fools who never saw your eyes,
Since you insist we are not one, but two.
Well, fifty years remain to jingle through
In which we will not meet, as you surmise;
And, after that dull masque has changed its guise,
Suppose we make the sun our rendezvous?

Naked and white and beautiful you stand,
Reining your fire-maned coursers with one hand,
And birds are in your laughter as you turn
That gaze of clear perfection to my own,
And meet the petal-kiss that seems to burn,
And makes us less divisible than stone!

TOAD AND WASP

I saw a toad
Was eating a wasp.
The wings glowed
In the fumbling grasp.

The sting thrust
At the mumbling mouth,
Bitter as dust
And hot as drouth.

The toad swallowed
And spat brown.
His belly hollowed
To take wasp down.

His throat wrinkled,
His eyes bulged out,
His skin crinkled
With lust and doubt.

Ants were a pleasure,
Mayflies sweet,
But wasp was a treasure
Too hot to eat.

He coughed faintly
Like death at a saint.
He looked quaintly.
He tasted paint.

Wasp lay buried
In a leather bag
But his sting still harried
The puzzled hag.

Life was a nagger
And Life had gone,
But the acid dagger
Still stung on.

Toad had a pout
Of pain and grief.
He spat wasp out
On a parsley leaf.

Wasp crawled away
In toad's spittle.
Wasp looked gray.
Wasp looked little.

Toad, unbeaten,
Observed the crawl.
Wasp might be eaten
After all.

His tongue extended,
He caught the bruised
Body, defended
By steel long-used.

IX THE ISLAND AND THE FIRE

THE ISLAND AND THE FIRE

HERE, on the pure verge of the outmost sand,
I heap the broken sticks that will be fire.

The tide is going out, out with the day.

I have known earth.
Water-veined earth, whose body we deliver
At harvest, with the sickle of the West,
With the hard music of a thousand reapers,
And I have seen
Under the beat of reapers, under the clean
Implacable knife-dance of the whirling steel,
The child arise, the sunlocked child be born
—White flesh of earth, flesh of the honeymeal
Not yet ground into bread between the stones—
The fields lie quiet then. The fields are sleepers.
Only the red moon gleans among the corn.
In the long shack the tired men do not stir,
Sleep is their sweat, sleep is their hair and bones,

[223]

Sleep heavy as an anvil, fierce as lust.
The earth has yielded, we are done with her,
Dust of the harvest, mid-American dust.
Yet, if you put your ear
Close by the stubble-spear,
Close to the wheel-tracked ground
On such a harvest night,
You still will hear the sound
That is its own delight,
The water-voice, the voice of the living river,
The blood of earth, still beating the torn breast.

And I have touched the clod
Of Indian soil, the clay baked into god,
So rough and light, so curiously warm,
Dry as the rattles of the rattlesnake
Under the arrow-heat,
Soil of the arrow, soil of the blue storm.
Such soils are magic, though they grow no wheat.
They hold the austere medicine of the waste,
The bitter sagebrush-taste,
The coyote-cry, the camp of solitude,
And when the slow-voiced Indian women make
Pots from such soil, the clay beneath the smooth,
Brown, powerful hand has, in its shaping, blind
Atoms of magic, atoms of the wind.
The yucca-flower is there,
The Gila-monster's tooth
Crushed to imperial dust,
The feathered gods of the land,
The glitter in the air,
The glitter from the sand,
The caked, wolf-trodden crust
By the dead water-hole,
All this within the bowl,
All this beneath the hand.

Take up the brush and ring
The red and black design
Around the savage thing
And sell it to a fool
For something quaint and crude—
No Eastern snows can cool
That fever of the dried-up watercourses,
And, though he fill it up with alien wine,
The cup from which he drinks
Was stained with fiercer inks
Than any grape gives back,
Dust of the panther-track,
Dust of the crumbled skulls of desert-horses.

2

I have taken earth
In Georgia and Vermont. I have taken the brown
Cake of the leaf-mold where the stream runs down,
I have gathered the first blood-root of the year
(Its frail stem smelling of loam.) I have seen the stripe
On the chipmunk's back and knelt by the Indian-pipe
In wet, green moss by the drinking-pool of the deer.

I have cut from the inland lawn
The bird-walked turf of dawn,
Matted, staining the knife, the strong roots hard to divide.
There was plenty where it grew.
It was square and heavy with dew.
It had fed the bee and the rose. I could not put it aside.

I have been drowned
In the red earth, deep in the three-cropped ground
Where any seed will bloom.
I have been buried in a richer tomb
Than any king's and risen with the seed.

My hands are stained with all the earth I have known.
My bone is the hard bone
Of the plow-breaking rock, my flesh the obdurate flesh
Of farmlands that the naked rains refresh,
Acres that wore the Morgan horses out
Though they were stubborn and the best of their breed,
Acres of the scant harvest and the toil.

And when, for the space of a day, for the space of a night,
The soft South wind has scattered the snow about;
When the black icicle of March lies broken,
Broken with light,
And the cloud trembles and the word is spoken,
It is my body that the thawing springs
Sluice with new silver and the melted North,
It is my winters that are driven forth
Like the diminished ice, before the pound
Of freshets, harrowing the fallow ground,
It is my barrenness your floods assoil,
Dove of the waters, dove of the grey wings.

3

O great processional!
Here, on the last bare outpost of the sand,
Here, on the edge of land,
I cast my banner and your banner down.
Monsters of earth, creatures and shapes and forms,
Fed at her seasons, watered by her storms,
I have adored you, I have followed you,
Like the heartstolen child
Who hears, to his defeat,
The swan-voice from the wilderness, the solitary call,
Sudden and piercing-clear
The death-horn of the year
And the new promise blown

By Autumn in the air
—Cold Autumn, loitering the windy wild
With his red hounds before him, giving tongue,
And at his girdle hung
Golden and living still, one shining tress of murdered
    Summer's hair—
And so must follow, follow through the town,
Only to wake at last, abandoned by the spell,
Alone and weary in a hostile street.
And why he followed, he can never tell
Although he knows that every step he trod
Seemed taken in the imprint of a god
And still within his breast
The bones cry out for rest,
Rest underneath a wheel of stars and music from the
    stone.

I know that search, I know
The bitter after-throe,
The beauty, the betrayal, and the chain,
And how stout heart and all-devising brain
Are but two cups of essences distilled
Out of a flower and a rotten bone
By the strange quicksalt of transmuting death,
And even the airy breath
No cloud-engendered stray
But a more ghostly clay,
Winged, but with dusted wings, spirit but spirit bound,
And royally but mortally in cloths of pollen wound.
Nevertheless, here by the ebbing tide,
I have lost earth; it is scattered out of my hand;
It is mixed with the pure, unbreeding grains of the sand,
With the slinger's stone, with the ridges of the cleaned
    shell.
This earth is cast. It is well.
This earth is past, and its pride.

4

So, as the equal night,
Descending, mingles heaven and the sea
In one great wave of darkness that the weak,
First stars of evening mark but cannot light,
And the great planets beam
But with the sunken gleam
Of sea-fire on a drowning sailor's cheek,
Darkness obscure and waste,
Darkness to touch and taste,
Unearthly, everywhere,
I feed my own scant fire with scraps the sea has torn
And blow on it to keep the embers bright.
Beyond is nothing, nothing but the roar
Of the black breaker striking the black shore,
And the wet wind that haunts the ocean-born.
But here, at last, the flame burns steadily.

O spirit, weary with the love of earth,
Broken beneath her riches,
Your wounds are bound at last, your wounds are healed
By fire and salt, by darkness and the tide;
Speak, speak, before you pass,
Creature of burning glass,
And tell me how I, too, may live my enemy beside
And in my heart that enemy, and yet without despair,
And from what star in heaven forged the metal of that shield
Against which every arm of earth is lifted up in vain?

No, no, it would not stay.
It was a spirit and departed so.
And, far away,
In the dim courtyard, where the iron stakes
Are hung with seven veils of pearly cold,
The young beast, Dawn, the hunting-leopard, wakes,
Hungry for the new gold.

My ring of fire sinks into the grey ash.
I have kept the night-watch. It is time to go
Down past the flood-line and the shelving brown,
Down where the wreck of darkness lies awash
In the fresh tide of morning, and the curled
Edge of the wave strikes down,
And cleanse upon a knife of hissing spray
This heavy body, born again to-day.

Spirit that watched, spirit that fled away,
The land-breeze strengthens now
On breast and throat and brow,
All ocean cannot scourge it out of me.
Morning returns, and with it brings the world,
But, for an hour, phantom, we were free.

THE END